Another Language

Another Language

Jeanne Braham

Photographs by Robert Floyd

Bauhan Publishing
Peterborough, New Hampshire
2012

All photos ©2012 Robert Floyd, with the exception of the photo on
page 54 - taken by Kathy LaCroix and used by permission.

ISBN: 9780872331501

Library of Congress Cataloging-in-Publication data:

Braham, Jeanne, 1940-
 Another language : profiles of service dogs and their people / by Jeanne Braham ;
photographs by Robert Floyd. -- 1st ed.
    p. cm.
 ISBN 978-0-87233-150-1 (pbk. : alk. paper)
1. Service dogs. 2. People with disabilities. I. Title.
 HV1569.6.B73 2012
 362.4'0483--dc23

                          2011050627

BAUHAN
PUBLISHING LLC
7 MAIN STREET PETERBOROUGH NEW HAMPSHIRE 03458

WWW.BAUHANPUBLISHING.COM
                    603-567-4430

Book designed by Sarah F. Bauhan
Typeset in Gudrun Zapf von Hesse's Nofret
Cover design by Henry James

                              Manufactured in South Korea

Contents

Dedicated to:
Basket, Bronson, Dandi, Freddy, Grace, Mercury,
Merlin, Ronnie, Rusty, Sooner, Waldo

Introduction

Another Language

It's a sunny, leaf-strewn autumn day in late 2009; an extraordinary crowd mills in the hallway outside the conference room in the Fitchburg, Massachusetts, Marriott. Even a casual bystander could differentiate this group from the usual tweedy academics or business suits that typically congregate here. For one thing, a number of people wheel expertly around in wheelchairs or motorized scooters. Others use canes or crutches for support. But most eye-catching are the beautifully behaved dogs that are sprinkled liberally through the crowd—some alertly watching their owners for the next cue, others lying patiently beside their companions while conversations buzz over their heads. Labrador Retrievers, Smooth-coated Collies, Golden Retrievers, a Standard Poodle, an Australian Labradoodle, several smaller terrier or spaniel type dogs appear, all wearing the distinctive red vest marked NEADS, the National Education for Assistance Dog Service. Founded in 1976 in rural, central Massachusetts, the mission of NEADS is to provide, through well-trained assistance dogs, independence to people who are disabled or deaf; to help children and adults who can benefit from the therapeutic value of a dog; and to assist special educators and therapists who work with disabled children or adults. It's a mouthful of diverse responsibilities for medium-sized canines, but the dogs are up to the task and still able to generate the warmth and attention that comes their way simply by being handsome and well-mannered.

Most hearing dogs are rescued from animal shelters throughout New England and they are trained in a specially equipped "apartment" (designed to mimic the home environment they will soon assume) on the NEADS campus. They learn to alert their hearing-impaired owners to the doorbell, the tea kettle, the telephone, and the smoke alarm.

They "report" the neighbor at the door, the paperboy collecting, the blueberry pie about to come out of the oven, or a less benign intrusion.

Most service dogs are donated as puppies by breeders throughout the country. They are trained to provide a wide variety of services, including acting as balance dogs for people-many of them combat veterans—who are learning to walk with prostheses or weaning themselves from cumbersome crutches; as service dogs who can open doors, shut off lights, retrieve dropped objects for people confined to wheelchairs; or as therapy, social, and ministry dogs, acting as ambassadors of safety and good will for those who need the comfort of their presence.

For those fortunate enough to be matched with a NEADS dog, an intensive two-week onsite training period helps to forge the bond between the client and his or her companion dog. They live on the NEADS campus in a fully accessible and well-equipped residence, learning how to work together as a team and practicing how to achieve the maximum benefits possible as an integrated unit. Once they pass a rigorous test, a graduation ceremony honoring their achievement follows.

The big doors to the conference room swing outward and in we go to take our seats. A full screen video machine translates what is being said on stage into a text for the hearing impaired. Although I have yet to hear a single bark, we are warned to turn off all our cell phones: should one go off, all the hearing dogs will respond simultaneously.

One by one the "teams" come to the stage to receive their diplomas. Five combat veterans lead the group of fourteen graduate teams, four matched with jet-black Labs, the fifth with a sleek, yellow Lab. Although their stories differ in specific lyrics, there is a through-running melodic line: the injury and subsequent hospitalizations and surgeries, the adjustments to civilian life, the transforming power of getting the dog, the gratitude expressed to breeders, trainers, and the army of volunteers who make NEADS work—many of whom are in the audience. After each story applause resonates throughout the room.

Two young women graduate with their therapy dogs. One, who works as an occupational therapist at Shrewsbury Nursing and Rehab

Center, explains that her gorgeous Golden Retriever, Sutton, not only brightens the lives of the elderly residents at the center, but brings joy to the rest of the staff. The other woman works at Cottage Hill Academy, a residential facility helping young women struggling to overcome severe trauma. Her yellow Lab, Cal, brings the power of healing to these troubled girls, she says, and one look at Cal's beatific face provides its own confirmation.

Perhaps most memorably, a young, blonde girl who uses a wheelchair, wheels slowly on stage. She speaks very few words. But she weaves her fingers into the soft ears of her patient black Lab, communicating her love for him in another, unmistakably clear, language. [We later identified the pair as Katherine Ryan and her service dog, Harrington. Katherine is pictured with her younger sister, Maeve, her puppy raiser, Lindsay Ward, and her mother, Deena Ryan, who graciously gave us permission to publish the photograph.]

I have seen moments of pure joy at many graduations. But this ceremony has a defining edge, for it brings together men and women

who have had the courage to begin a whole new chapter of their lives with dogs who have demonstrated their capacity for rigorous training and the sensitivity to bond with their partners in uniquely beneficial ways. Neither could truly excel without the other, a truth everybody in the room affirms.

My admiration for and desire to write about assistance dogs and their human partners follows a rather circuitous route, aspects of which I discovered only in the process of writing this book. While I've always loved dogs, I've never had any professional training, nor have I ever been paired with a dog who mastered anything more than the basic "sit," "stay," "heel," "come" commands. To learn that dogs could be trained to respond to more than two dozen commands was a revelation. But clearly, several personal experiences prompted me to want to know more about assistance dogs and their vital work. The first was the example of my father, a dog-loving small town lawyer who bought "seventy-two acres of wilderness" in northwestern Pennsylvania with his mustering-out pay from the Army and spent the next two decades clearing the land and building a summer cottage atop its steepest hill. My older sister and I were installed none too enthusiastically on that remote outpost during our teen years. But his enthusiasm was infectious as was his great dream of breeding and training seeing eye dogs when he reached retirement age. As fate would have it, he never reached retirement age, felled by a massive heart attack when I was still in college. But his dream lingered in my mind.

Years later, my sister was diagnosed with ALS, often called Lou Gehrig's disease, a cruel motor-neuron disease that paralyzes the muscles in the body while leaving the mind perfectly lucid. I cared for her, with the help of others, in the last year of her life, a period marked by the steady progression of the disease: from cane to walker to motorized wheelchair. I witnessed her frustration when she dropped her phone or her wallet—and her helplessness when she took one of the sudden, unanticipated falls that characterize that disease. I remember taking her to the local mall in a portable wheelchair, the stares of the curious, and her experience, as we plunged into the crowds, of being "waist high in the world," as it's described by Nancy Mairs, the essayist who has written so discerningly about navigating the world with debilitating MS. I wished for her a greater measure of help than I could provide. A decade later, I cared for my mother in my home for four years prior to her death at the age of 101. The challenges of the disabled became a real part of my daily life—and yet I realized that I, like many others, had little awareness and even less information about the support and services assistance dogs can provide.

One day, quite by accident, I saw a wiggly black Lab puppy at the local supermarket. He was out on a weekend socialization furlough and was wearing a tiny but striking crimson vest emblazoned: NEADS. I had found my "true subject," that phrase Patricia Hampl uses to describe an idea that has percolated in the consciousness of a writer long before she realizes it.

My partner in this endeavor, Robert Floyd, contributed not only his skills as a professional photographer, his "other language," but a hands-on grasp of the subject. He is raising two Australian Labradoodles who are training to be therapy dogs; his experience with their training, as well as his fascination with human-canine bonds, added depth and detail to my observations.

We decided to tell this story by profiling and photographing a number of human-canine teams who have graduated from NEADS quite recently. Interviews with a breeder of therapy dogs, staff and trainers at NEADS, a weekend puppy raiser, and an inmate dog trainer serve to frame and put into context the primary stories. Insofar as possible I've allowed the subjects to speak in their own words. While this is a book describing some of the cutting-edge programs and expanding services now available in the world of assistance dogs, it is, in a more intimate way, a group of intensely personal stories told from the inside of difficult and challenging experiences.

Chapter One

This is What Disability Looks Like

Kathy White and Freddy

Out of the corner of my eye I see the car arrive and, despite the rain-slick parking lot, a compactly built woman and her long-legged Lab make their way confidently to the front door of the NEADS training center. Freddy, the black Lab, is wearing a red backpack with a lightweight grip on top and his owner, Kathy White, strides along, holding the grip in one hand and a walking stick in the other. They could be heading out to hike on a portion of the Appalachian Trail. Instead, Kathy has agreed to meet me at NEADS, equidistant from our respective homes, to tell her story and demonstrate some of the things Freddy is able to do for her.

Freddy obviously remembers the place well: his ears cock in the direction of the kennels, his nose explores the familiar smells on the floor, and he greets the housekeeper with undisguised joy.

Kathy is equally at home, and as we settle into the conference room for our conversation she promises Robert a tour of the campus and a working demonstration of Freddy's skills in the upstairs training arena.

She begins:

Animals have always been a part of my life. My mother grew up on a farm in northwestern Pennsylvania and as kids we used to go to visit the cow barns. Of course we came home always wanting a cow, hardly a realistic possibility in our neighborhood. But we did have sheep and dogs and cats when I was growing up and I seem to have had some sort of fuzzy thing in my adult homes always."

In fact it was during my search for a Newfoundland dog, a large dog that could help me with my balance, that I happened to find NEADS. Here was one of the largest national training centers for assistance dogs

in the United States, right in my backyard. And yes, they train balance and mobility dogs, hearing dogs, therapy dogs, service dogs for the wheelchair-bound—the list is vast. Ministry dogs: that caught my eye, since volunteerism and ministry work are vital parts of what I do. Was this possible? For me?

So I applied. And applied. And applied, for about a four-year period. The process began with a prescription from a doctor (I got two for Ménière's disease and fibromyalgia), continued with a lengthy application form summarizing my life experience, and completed with an extensive interview. I was asked during the interview what I wanted the dog to help me accomplish in my life. And I took a deep breath and replied honestly: I needed physical help with my daily life and I also need a dog sensitive enough and well-mannered enough to be a partner in my ministry.

NEADS said yes.

What I didn't entirely realize at that time was how special my dog would need to be. Because of my balance problems I would need a large dog, one whose back I could comfortably reach to steady myself. NEADS doesn't train large-breed dogs like English Mastiffs or Newfies or Great Danes—they are too short-lived and their working life, since service dogs train for about two years before beginning to work, is quite abbreviated. I would need to wait for a "large boned" dog of a medium-sized breed, like a Lab or Poodle or Golden Retriever.

My dual expectations for the dog also complicated the picture. Service dogs have different personalities than therapy or ministry dogs. By their nature service dogs must be intensely bonded to "their person," listening without flinching to whatever they are asked to do. In contrast, a ministry dog, though bonded to his or her master, is more comfortable in group settings, more outgoing and social. I was asking for both.

I knew it would be a long wait to put this constellation of things together. But I couldn't really give up on either of my needs. Clearly, my disabilities were not going away and my gravitation toward the ministry had been a slow, incremental evolution that I wanted to honor.

My physical symptoms came in tandem with each of my pregnancies, a not-unusual occurrence I later learned. I was diagnosed with fibromyalgia when I was pregnant with my now nearly twenty-one-year-old daughter. As most people know from the TV ads, FM is characterized by pain, sometimes in the joints, sometimes all over the body, and by the crushing fatigue it produces. Since I've had this condition for some time, I've gained some understanding of how to manage it. But FM is notoriously unpredictable and some days are just better than others, despite my best efforts. Days like these [she points to the cold rain falling outside] are hard, just as winter is much tougher than spring and summer.

Shortly after the birth of my son, I was diagnosed with Ménière's disease, a condition of the inner ear that causes dizziness and for me a sudden loss of balance, without warning, usually at just the worst moment. I've taken some spectacular falls, some funny and some not so funny. Once when hiking with my son's Cub Scout troop in the hills of central Massachusetts I fell off the top of one sizable hill, sliding feet first down the long slope and into a major mud puddle. The older scouts took their cue from my son, who after determining that I was okay, laughed, but some others looked at me with utter dismay. Other times I was not so lucky and once pitched forward on an asphalt driveway, landing directly on my head. While I sometimes kid that Ménière's gives the term "dizzy dame" new definition, I knew I had to take steps to protect myself and my young children—especially after I became a single mom—from the accidents it might cause.

I've lived with both of these conditions for more than eighteen years, and although I've always carried a cane (I used to call it "my teenagers' shin-whacker"), people invariably say, "You don't look disabled."

"What does disabled look like?" I always counter. "It doesn't always mean crutches, prostheses, motorized chairs. THIS is what disabled looks like." You know, I think that's one of the biggest challenges I face as a member of the invisibly disabled. I don't look "other."

"I can be pretty determined when I need to be, and I decided to complete my college education, even with a very young daughter and another child soon on the way. I applied to Wheaton College in Massachusetts, not knowing where the tuition money would come from. They had a continuing education program for "geriatric students" like me and although it took me three years to finish, I did, concentrating on religion and philosophy courses and doing intensive research on Holocaust survivors and the lives they led after the camps were liberated. I think I might have entered seminary thereafter, if I had not had reservations about subjecting my young kids to the scrutiny of being "preacher's kids." I've always been very active in church life and it seems to me that preachers' kids often suffer by being held to a higher standard than other kids their age. I didn't want that experience for my kids, so I just moved into the work force.

Well, the months awaiting a match passed, then years passed. I was

matched briefly with a Standard Poodle, but the bond was not a good one and I felt guilty asking for more time with that dog since others, particularly those afflicted with allergies or asthma, could benefit from a hypo-allergenic dog. Then one day about a year ago I was asked to assume the children's ministry in my church. I told my pastor "yes" on Sunday, November 30. The very next day, Monday, December 1, NEADS called to say they thought they had a match for me. And I met Freddy. I knew quickly that we'd make a fine team. Within a week and a half I knew he would come instantly when I called him, ready to help with whatever I needed.

Freddy has an interesting past, I discovered, since he was a "reject" from Guiding Eyes for the Blind. As I understand it, they were able to do an evaluation at an early age and determined that Freddy would never be able to "intelligently disobey" his master, a crucial need for a seeing eye dog. [Intelligent disobedience means deliberately ignoring a given command if that command would put the team in harm's way: the most likely example is crossing a busy street when the dog sees danger.]

Most training organizations have reciprocal agreements with one another, the sort of arrangement that Guiding Eyes for the Blind maintains with NEADS. If a dog is inappropriate for one program, the other organization will evaluate the dog in accordance with the needs of its program. Good canine "capital" is a rare and precious thing; since the need is so great, assistance dog organizations are banding together to make sure every avenue is explored before any dog "flunks out." In Freddy's case, the loss to Guiding Eyes was a gain to NEADS—and especially to me.

Freddy spent some time at a very early age at the Puppy House at NEADS, then went for some basic training with an inmate at the Hampshire County House of Correction. On weekends Freddy was with his puppy raisers, Laura and Lenny Kokoski. We've remained in touch and during our training at the Meet and Greet, Lenny and Laura presented me with a "puppy book" full of pictures of Freddy growing up and going to various places for socialization. They did a fabulous job, since there is very little Freddy encounters that makes him anxious.

Another important influence in Freddy's young life came from John Moon, the director of communications at NEADS. John let Freddy live under his desk at NEADS, teaching him how to behave in an office environment. Now Freddy is completely quiet under the desk in my office and my office mates often don't realize there's a dog in our midst until I take him for a drink of water.

Christy Bassett was Freddy's trainer, and consequently mine, too. Her low-key approach is amazing—and dogs fall all over themselves trying to do things for her. When I first met Freddy it was clear he was tolerating me for Christy's sake. I tried not to be disappointed that my new friend wasn't bowled over by my endearments, but Christy told me he would adjust and that our bond would be strong and utterly reliable. How right she was.

Of course, Freddy is still quite young and I'm mindful that he needs play time and plenty of exercise. At work I arrive half an hour early so that I can give him some special attention at noontime. There's a walking path at work we can use and a nearly vacant hall with a smooth floor just made for sliding a toy on. His great love, however, is speed: he loves to run. So I try to give him open space at least once a week to run like crazy, usually at a playgroup, where he loves to be chased by other dogs. He's become a master tease, trying to engage the other dogs in play.

One of the things I think all teams learn is that we're in this for life and I try to be vigilant about nipping bad habits in the bud before they're full-blown problems. I'm also careful to keep Freddy's training "fresh" by using all his commands.

He braces me to stand up from a chair without pitching forward or falling; he fetches things I drop so that I don't risk falling over. He can turn lights on and off, and he opens HP-assist doors by pushing with his paws on the pressure pad. He can tug doors open too, if I put a rope on the handle. (I put a rope on my home refrigerator door, since it sometimes sticks. But when my son saw the Budweiser commercial where the dog tugs open the refrigerator door and delivers a beer,

suddenly Freddy was seen in a whole new light.) He retrieves his own leash and hands it to me, especially when HE is ready for a walk. On tough days Freddy wears a harness to help steady me as I walk.

"What would happen," I interject, "if you went completely down. Could Freddy help you get to your feet?"

"Yes, there's a technique for that. And if I were hurt, unable to stand back up, here's what we'd do." Kathy makes a sudden movement with her right hand, tapping her left upper chest area, right about at the clavicle. Instantly Freddy, who has uttered not a sound, barks a sharp piercing bark. Kathy gestures a second time, and again Freddy barks urgently.

"That's the alert signal and it never fails to generate some help," she says, as Freddy settles into a "stay" at her feet.

I also knew quite quickly that Freddy would be a good ministry dog. Since an autistic boy trained with his dog in our class I knew Freddy was meant for a youth ministry just by watching how he responded to this young man's awkward and enthusiastic love with gentleness and affection. Freddy has since proved to be a loving and welcome addition to our church family, ministering to any child within reach—no matter what age.

Sundays are days of special excitement for Freddy. Not only does he have two adult congregants who offer enormous amounts of affection to him, we've also spent some time with a class for developmentally challenged adults. Several members of this class were afraid of dogs for one reason or another, and it has been a triumph to watch Freddy win over several hearts of previous fearful adults and children. One adult wants to greet Freddy whenever he sees him, a huge change in his demeanor. Two others in this class, good friends, get very excited to interact with Freddy. Their mother watches in amazement. It's been a lesson for me in the power of acceptance and unconditional love, freely given and freely received.

Three or four children surround Freddy and look forward each Sunday to spending time with him between Sunday school and church.

Oftentimes their stories of beloved pets tumble out as they share time with Freddy. And he has a special place in the hearts of the children who participate in the divorce ministry, often a different group from the Sunday regulars. I let Freddy take the lead to find the hurting soul who needs my attention, child or adult. His instinct is amazing and trustworthy. I've come to realize that it was hardly a coincidence that just one day after I offered to volunteer for the divorce ministry, NEADS called to match me with Freddy.

Under the American with Disabilities Act, churches are exempt from the requirement to allow service animals access to the premises. When I visit a new church, I need to call ahead to ask if Freddy will be welcome. But my home church has welcomed service dogs in training for quite a while, so there was no hesitation when we became a team. I think the pastor and elders realize how much Freddy enhances the work that I do, even when it takes on a "creative cast." For example, not too long ago a fourteen-year-old member of one of my groups was diagnosed with non-Hodgkin's lymphoma. She was required to make weekly trips into Boston for chemo treatments. Freddy and I would, of course, have visited her, had her immunity system not been so compromised. So instead, Freddy has been "writing notes" to her, to cheer her spirits and remind her that there are better days ahead.

You know, sooner or later people begin to pigeon-hole you because of your disability. "Kathy shouldn't do this, Kathy can't do that." And of course disabilities vary greatly. But I've found that you can either become your disability or you can move past it. I observe the boundaries that I have to respect, but I don't let my disabilities prohibit me from doing what I love to do.

I love the water, for example, and being out on the water in a canoe or kayak is a source of great peace for me. Okay, do you get the picture? Here's a woman with no balance teetering in a canoe or kayak. It's amazing how much water you can take on without sinking. But I laugh. I get soaking wet. My kids laugh. And after all, I'm matched with the perfect water dog.

Freddy and I have been together a year now. I'm conscious of the wonderful foundation NEADS has provided for us, but I'm also conscious of our responsibilities as a team—to one another and to others. As we go about our daily lives, I take the time to educate people everywhere we go. When people see us in a store and I overhear their comments, I'll always take the opportunity to open up a conversation. I find the vast majority of people, at least in our area, are well informed about service dog etiquette and are genuinely interested in learning what Freddy does. Because we are an anomaly, we have become de facto ambassadors, so there is some weight, self-imposed I know, to act well and pave the way for other service teams. Sometimes we make mistakes or have a little accident, of course, but I hope we are examples not only of the value of one dog in one life, but of the value of opening your heart to the animals with whom we all share kinship.

Relating to an animal changes the human dynamic. Freddy's friends are free to offer him affection and love, without rebuff or rejection. On Freddy's part, there are no expectations and no challenges, other than the simple expectation and trust that he will be treated with kindness and respect, to be cared for and loved. That's a brand of comfort that humans oftentimes can only aspire to offer each other. Walls come down, bonds develop. Freddy acts, in brief moments, as a conduit through which deep feelings flow and I am privy to private struggles and trials and triumphs, personal stories that otherwise wouldn't be shared were it not for Freddy's presence.

Having Freddy beside me every day is an amazing journey. It's been a year, and the sense of awe has yet to diminish.

I hope it never does.

Chapter Two

Life Is What You Make It

Bob Swain and Waldo

Even though Bob Swain is juggling our meeting with introductions to a new personal care attendant, it's easy to see that he's a "take charge guy," someone accustomed to the complex troubleshooting required in his former job as an engineer and a skill useful as he pursues a new career as a CPA. He maneuvers his power chair deftly around the Burlington condo he shares with his wife, Marie, and Waldo, a sleek black Lab, who has been his service dog for the past year and a half. Waldo settles himself at Bob's feet as Bob begins to relate his life story. For most of us, the story would be almost too dramatic to summarize, but Bob lays out each episode as if he were overturning a finite number of face cards in the hand he was dealt.

I was very sick as a child, suffering bouts of paralysis: First, I was diagnosed with polio along with my mother during the terrible epidemic in the 1950s. I was about two years old at the time and had to wear braces. Then from the ages of thirteen to fifteen I spent long stretches in the hospital, felled by Guillain Barré disease, an inflammation of the spinal cord that rendered me a quad. I couldn't even tolerate having sheets on my body. Although I recovered from both of those illnesses I was aware that I might well inherit hereditary spastic paraplegia (HSP), since the disease afflicted my father and two uncles and eventually also my younger brother. HSP is a condition characterized by a progressive lower extremity weakness and spasticity. While no two people experience HSP in quite the same way, mine was a gradual disability, progressing from the age of thirty-five. Now, at the age of fifty-seven, I use a power chair with all its attendant challenges; additionally, a stroke in 2007 affected my speech and my arm and hand strength slightly.

Despite the health setbacks, I was always an organized, hard-driving guy. I have a commercial pilot's FAA license in gliding, with private privileges in single engine planes. I have an amateur radio technician's license and was certified as a State Police firearms instructor. After Marie and I met and married in the 1980s, we traveled extensively. And after graduating from college I held a series of progressively more advanced jobs in engineering, working with major international companies.

Marie, too, went to college, but in September of 2000, right after she graduated from a program at Boston University, she was in a horrific car accident. Hit head-on by an unlicensed seventeen-year-old driver, she shattered all the bones in her right foot and fractured seven bones in her leg. She came close to losing her leg. I cared for her during her recovery and through ten surgeries, and that experience gave me a perspective on what it feels like to be a caregiver, as well as what it feels like now to receive care.

Perhaps the one blow I hadn't anticipated, job discrimination, knocked the wind out of my sails, at least for a time. I fell victim to one of the oldest forms of job discrimination known in the corporate world: I was assigned a job I could not perform. I had worked for a large international company for six years without complaint, when I was told that in order to continue I'd have to be able to move thirty to fifty pound objects independently. At first I was devastated by the bald inequity of it all. But then I got busy. I consulted with advisers at three bureaus throughout the state and spent long hours on the Internet retrieving information on disability discrimination. Before I knew it, I had filled a three-inch binder with documentation and legal strategy. I became a not-so-pretend paralegal through this process. In the end, through mediation, I was able to win a six-figure settlement enabling me to achieve a mid-career change by going to college and learning a new profession. I also felt strongly about not draining Marie's funds for her retirement, money she has earned and deserves to keep for her old age.

You know, since I've been in this chair and perhaps even more since I've gotten Waldo, I've become more in touch with other people's feelings. Maybe more comes my way, or maybe I probe a bit more?

For example, I learned much from my former personal care attendant, who came from Rwanda. She lost her husband and her father in the genocide there. We would talk a lot about the cards life deals to you and she was someone who taught me to see the folly of living in the past. What good does it do to hate a race or hate a company? Close the book on the past and put your assets into the future. Life is what you make of it.

The light is fading in this late autumn afternoon and Bob offers to take us to the recreation clubhouse in the condo complex so that Robert can get some good photos in natural light. Waldo is happy at the prospect of getting outside and stands right up to the chair as Bob puts on his working gear. As we travel the distance to the clubhouse, Bob tells us the story of acquiring Waldo from NEADS.

Marie and I had a little nine-pound Min-Pin, Sadie, who had been with us for many, many years. I took her everywhere with me, even up in the glider. And in the years when I was bouncing around from doctor to doctor, trying to manage chronic pain without adequate medication, Sadie served, in her own way, as my service dog. Her special function was helping me get through the nights. But by the time I was thinking of applying to NEADS, Sadie was quite old and almost blind, and Marie and I worried a great deal about a service dog's impact on her life.

A client at NEADS is also expected to contribute or raise a substantial amount of money to defray some of the expensive and extensive training his or her dog receives. So that was another major consideration.

And perhaps I also had some reservations in acknowledging my need for a service dog: after all, progressive diseases make you move from a cane to a chair and now to a chair with a dog. I had to learn to see a service dog as just another "tool," one that would help me do the things I still wanted to do with my life.

But I really had no idea how central Waldo would become in my life, or very little notion of this huge network of people who contribute to the training of a service dog. He fundamentally changes the way I am seen and the way I see myself.

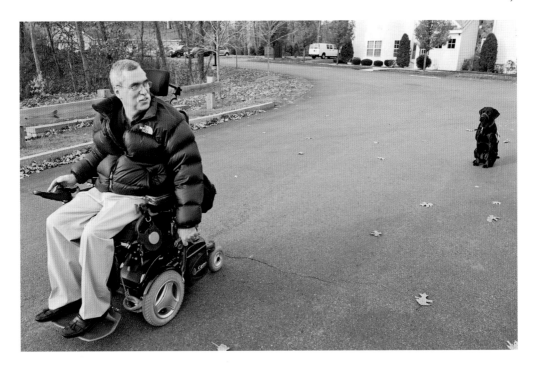

When you're viewed by society as "Disabled Person" your self-image changes. I require people to help me get dressed, drive me to appointments, pick up things I've dropped, open doors. And in the past many people would address questions about me to my care attendant: "Where does he live?" "Does he want a drink of water?" Every time that happened I lost a little more of my identity. But then Waldo came into my life.

The NEADS staff coordinated a breeder, trainers, handlers, volunteers, donors, all of whom played a part in creating the incredible service dog Waldo is today. The Prison PUP Program readied Waldo to learn not only obedience skills, but specialized skills like opening doors, turning off lights, picking up dropped objects. Volunteers brought Waldo into their communities to teach him about busy roads and public transportation and crying babies and noisy vacuum cleaners. He was taught that all people can be trusted to keep him safe and give him love, even when his strongest bond will be with one individual.

So when Waldo came to me and gave me his trust and respect,

I found my trust in and respect for myself returning each day. All people who navigate life in wheelchairs have stories about who stared at them for endless minutes, or who crossed the street in order to avoid passing them on the sidewalk. When I'm out with Waldo, his admirable obedience and quick response to commands draws attention to us. We are sought out now, not avoided.

We pause at the front door of the Clubhouse. To the right is a large fitness room with the usual array of exercise machines, spinner bikes, and weights. "Let me show you how I exercise Waldo," Bob says, his mustache twitching with barely concealed amusement. He finds the key to the treadmill machine, motions for Waldo to jump on board, then punches in a code. Waldo runs flawlessly, as if in a Nike ad.

Waldo also became a cause célèbre at Bob's recent induction into Phi Theta Kappa, a national honor society at Middlesex Community College, where Bob has maintained a sterling GPA over the past two years. "At first they said that Waldo couldn't go up onto the stage when I received the award," Bob said, adding, with a slight smile, "so I said, no Waldo, no Bob." Waldo was proudly on stage.

Waldo also accompanies Bob to the ninth floor of Spalding Rehab Hospital in Boston, the place where Bob convalesced after his stroke.

That floor contains patients with spinal cord injuries, stroke and brain injuries, and often the patients don't have many visitors. It can be a lonely place and Waldo is welcome there, for he can pick up articles patients have dropped while I chat with them. There is lots for me to learn too as my condition progresses, so we all help one another.

One of my goals is to participate in the Cigna Falmouth Road Race. In 2008 and 2009 Waldo and I were asked to come down to a booth at the registration center for this race—the one on the Cape that supports so many worthy charitable causes, including NEADS. We talked to many people, attempting to give our face and our name to the value and importance of service dogs. That's important work and we'll go again this year in that capacity. Although I realize my physical challenges, my hope is to be able to compete in the race in the future. For the last two years I have been using a hand-cranked adaptive bicycle at the Spaulding Rehabilitation Hospital. This bicycle

allows individuals with disabilities to gain and maintain overall health through the use of adaptive equipment. Waldo likes to get out and run alongside me to stay in shape, so I think it would be pretty exciting if we could participate together.

Bob and Waldo's training regimen was interrupted six weeks before their first planned attempt to compete in the race, however.

While reaching for some clothes in a bedroom closet I took a dramatic fall into the closet door. Waldo came rushing to my side and luckily Marie was at home as well. I knew, given my pain level, that I would need greater assistance than they could provide, so I pushed the medical alert button attached to my wrist and asked the dispatcher for help.

Waldo went with me in the ambulance and Marie followed in the car as quickly as possible. The Emergency Room was very crowded that evening and since Waldo practically got run over on a couple of occasions we decided that Marie should take him home until I was admitted to the hospital. Just as the sun was beginning to come up I was finally transferred to a room. An orthopedist examined me and told me I had ripped a rotator cuff in my left shoulder and broken a rib on my left side as well.

When I talked with Marie we decided that she'd take Waldo to work with her until I got transferred to rehab—and he'd join me there. Every day after work Marie and Waldo would visit me and within a week's time I was transferred to a rehabilitation hospital. I realized that serious physical and occupational therapy lay ahead for me and I asked if Waldo could be with me during this process.

At first I encountered some resistance, since some of the nursing staff had had negative experiences with dogs in their countries of origin. But I learned long ago that you have to respect people's responses and differing cultural experiences if you expect to earn their respect in return. So we took every opportunity to talk and to compare how their experiences of the undomesticated dogs in their native countries— where they are kept largely as attack animals—differed from highly trained, positively reinforced service dogs.

As they lost their fear of Waldo they often made a point to come in to see him—and me, in the bargain. I feel certain I gained more attention from the nursing staff because Waldo was by my side.

Of course, I had to be responsible for Waldo's care: I had to maneuver into a wheelchair to get him outside, to make sure he had food, water, exercise. But these responsibilities gave me the incentive to work harder on my therapy, just as Waldo's presence lightened the lives of many patients on our corridor who stopped to chat and pat the dog.

It takes some concerted effort to introduce a service dog into a hospital setting. But the rewards were obvious: for me, for Waldo, for many of my nurses, and for those patients who encountered us on our walks. I urge others to consider taking their service dogs with them when hospitalized, if they are physically able to be responsible for the dog's care.

Waldo and I are back home now, and the Falmouth Race is out there for next year, beckoning.

Chapter Three

Amazing Grace

Beth Lewis and Grace

Perhaps because I had heard so many stories about "Amazing Grace," the beautiful Golden Retriever who overcame very long odds to become a uniquely successful therapy dog, I think I half-expect her to come through the NEADS front door supported on a portable throne. Instead, she trots in with her partner, psychologist Beth Lewis, performs a perfect sit/stay and then, when released, runs to greet several of her old friends on the NEADS staff. She's a beauty, with a honey-red wavy coat, beautiful head, and ease of movement that belies the three major surgeries she's endured (with, perhaps, a fourth still to go). Grace's journey is unique: for most canine-human teams, the human partner is the disabled one. Grace's early life experience reversed those roles. But others stepped in to save her and, in ways we may never entirely understand, Grace has translated her own struggles into greater empathy for others.

Beth, who shares Grace's luminous hair color, settles at the conference table with Grace at her feet.

I am a weekend puppy raiser, one of those folks who volunteer to pick a puppy up at the prison where he or she is being trained, and then spends the weekend introducing the dog to new sights and sounds and smells. Typically we go to malls, for walks in the woods, to my young nieces' sporting events—in short, to all the places the puppy can never experience inside a prison setting. Grace was the second puppy I had worked to socialize. China, my first dog, ultimately went as a service dog to a veteran from Tennessee; Grace came to me shortly after China left. She was named by [puppy raiser] Bonnie Pansa's special education class, which raised the $1,000 necessary to name her. And did they do a good job!

Soon into her training I began to realize that Grace had problems: she never wanted to play fetch or run like other dogs, she couldn't get in or out of my car with any ease, and she was insecure on stairs. Her first inmate handler, Sheldon, also saw Grace's limitations and, after he was instructed to keep Grace as quiet as possible, began to carry her up and down the steep steps in the prison. We voiced our concerns to the NEADS staff, they took a set of X-rays, and sure enough: Grace had severe hip dysplasia. Some months later with another set of X-rays we discovered she had significant arthritis in both elbows. For a time I thought she would be deemed a "fabulous flunkie," the term NEADS uses to denote a puppy who may have marvelous traits, but for health or other reasons cannot complete the training program. But instead, NEADS took custody of her and planned for the surgeries. After her first surgery the NEADS chief operating officer, Candi Hitchcock, took Grace in and thereafter she was allowed to recuperate with me. She has bounced back after each of her surgeries and since she accompanies me to both of my work settings—I teach at Rhode Island College and offer therapy at a nearby clinic on weekends—she has developed into a superb therapy dog. If all goes as planned, we'll graduate in March.

While Grace settles in with a large stuffed bone, I ask Beth how she got interested in NEADS.

Well, that's a layered answer, I guess. Dogs have always occupied a special place in my life. For example, when I was growing up we had two dogs. Even though I had a brother and a sister, everybody kind of accepted that the dogs were "mine" and I certainly gave them all my attention. First I had a Collie and then a German Shepherd mix, Thunder. He was very special. I knew from about the age of seven that I carried a kind of sadness within and I'd take Thunder for long walks in the woods; he would comfort me. During my college and graduate school days, dogs weren't an option, though I had cats. But when I was employed as a psychologist at the University of Massachusetts Medical School, I found my opportunity to not only have a dog in my life, but to give back something vital to somebody else. I was working with

adolescents in an intensive residential treatment program. And if a kid achieved a certain level in the program, he or she was given the opportunity to work at NEADS, helping socialize the puppies, walking the dogs, doing basic obedience training. That's how I learned first about the program, and later I collected information on how to be a weekend puppy raiser.

Once Grace was with me and I saw her special qualities, she began accompanying me to classes and therapy sessions. In fact, she accompanies me just about everywhere. I often visit my sister who has two girls. Her youngest, Olivia, loves Grace with a passion and Grace loves her back just as hard. Each time Livvy leaves the room and then comes back in Grace will act as if it's the first time she's seen her: euphoria. And she does the same thing with my clients, welcoming them, wagging her tail, picking up a toy to share it with them. For clients who are struggling, Grace's welcome makes them feel special, noticed, appreciated. If a client has no interest in her, Grace will lie

quietly at my feet. But if she senses sadness or despair and a client accepts her, she will go and lie right next to them, often putting her head on their feet or sometimes their lap. Her presence is enormously comforting. Often clients will just stroke her and those who need to cry, cry, just as those who need to smile, smile.

She's also a very important tool I use with my students, for often Grace can model concepts I'm trying to teach them like behavioral analysis, positive reinforcement, and shaping. I teach a course in behavior modification, for example, and typically I'll have one or two students in the class who are afraid of dogs. I'll check with any students before I use them as an example, and if they're willing I'll use Grace to help me demonstrate how that fear can be conquered, the steps one can take to desensitize and ultimately modify behavior. When they see a concept translated into action something really clicks. They "get it," and Grace is the reason why.

They also love her, of course, and enable her habit of loving to push rocks around on the floor using her nose. If I try to intervene and take the rock away, they will advocate fiercely for her. Grace, the rock pusher, provides many moments of comic relief. Her nose has even become discolored from her love of pushing rocks. Since I am the clinical director of the Chemical Dependency and Addictions degree program, many of my students stay with me for two years. Students in this program graduate with a BA in psychology and a BS in chemical dependency. They learn counseling techniques and also complete an internship. So we get to know one another quite well and Grace has her built-in fan club.

Grace is also an important "demonstrating tool" in my therapy work. For example, I work with a little seven-year-old girl who can't calm herself down. So when she comes in for her sessions, we get Grace very excited, playing with blocks and balls, jumping on mats, running and tugging. And then, together, we calm Grace down. We practice this over and over again, until she can learn to apply the same techniques to herself.

Or another example might be the eighteen-year-old who has Asperger's that I work with. This client can't identify emotions, can't read the cues in the eyes, the face, the body language that signal what someone is feeling. So we practice on Grace. I'll say, "Look at Grace. Does she want to play? Does she want to lie down? Does she look sad? How do we know? "So you see Grace is absolutely central to the work I do. She may not function as a typical service dog, but she assists me in every conceivable facet of my life.

I also volunteer to teach in the alternative sentencing program called "Changing Lives Through Literature." You may have heard of it, for it started right here in Massachusetts, then spread throughout New England and beyond. When a person is judged guilty of any nonviolent crime the sitting judge can impose an alternative sentence that he or she feels is an appropriate corrective: sometimes anger management, sometimes a domestic violence group, or this program, Changing Lives through Literature. A group of six-to-eight people ranging in age from adolescents to the middle-aged meets either every two weeks for twelve weeks, or every week for six weeks, and we read and discuss pieces of literature—novels sometimes in the longer interval sessions and usually short stories if the class meets every week. The pieces of fiction are chosen because they reflect the decision-making process and the consequences that follow. So our discussion centers around judgments, making responsible decisions.

I favor the classes that meet every week, for I find they promote a team feeling much more quickly. By the time we've been meeting every week for six weeks, everybody knows everybody else pretty well, has formed good attachments, and the participants tend to keep in touch with one another, just as the program does follow-up work, checking on the progress each person is making. Students are encouraged to get their GED, to apply to a community college, to go after a job, to keep setting and meeting goals.

I always begin with asking them about their values. I offer a handout listing maybe one hundred values that people in current society can hold and they are asked to choose which ones they care about most. Almost invariably all of them pick, among their top five values, "family." The sad truth is that most of them don't have supportive families, yet they want, they crave this kind of connection. And so teamwork, a sense of belonging to a larger, supportive mini-community, fills a very important void for them.

Grace goes with me to all of these meetings, working her special magic. And it is a marvelous teaching experience, not only because the material prompts a rare kind of candor, but because all the relationships that are formed are going to result in growth—for them and certainly for me. And Grace has that intuitive radar, even in these settings. In one group I had a young man who said almost nothing in the first session. He had had the tragic experience of drinking and driving and a passenger in his car, his best friend, was killed. Grace watched him in the first session and then she went right over to him and lay her head in his lap. Each session thereafter, she sat right by him; theirs was a visibly strong bond.

When the group completes the program, they make a written or oral presentation to the judge, describing what the program meant to them. This last class that I taught made a video, where each class member talked to the judge—and by extension, to each other—about what he or she had learned. And you know this experience changes their view of the law, too. At first they see the judge as some sort of ogre, imposing something boring or punitive on them. But by the end, the judge is smiling, shaking their hand, handing them a certificate marking their accomplishment. It changes their concept of "justice."

I've often thought about Grace's special gifts—her empathic capacities, her strength, her joie de vivre. And I believe Grace is the dog she is because of her own struggles. Perhaps that's a lesson we could all apply to ourselves. I, for example, have fought severe depression for over twenty-five years. That sadness I knew as early as the age of seven, helped only by my dog Thunder, grew into clinical depression by the time I was in college. I've endured a number of hospitalizations, starting in my college years—interruptions in graduate school stretching my doctorate into a ten-year process. I suspect I've tried about every "remedy" for depression available, including a range of medications, fish oil, a light box, electroconvulsive therapy. That last treatment mode was moderately helpful, but it carries one side effect for some people that I couldn't afford: short term memory loss—some people can't remember what happened six months before ECT. Of course, for a teacher and therapist, memory is crucial. So I simply couldn't risk that possibility and had to stop that course of treatment. When Grace came into my life I found her intuitive capacities comforting, her ability to connect with my clients and students instructive, and she, quite simply, made me laugh.

About a year ago I became part of a pilot program measuring the effectiveness of a vagus nerve stimulator, or VNS. The year passed and the clinical trial is over, but the VNS continues its work. It is much like a pacemaker with electrodes that extend into my brain. It emits an electric pulse for thirty seconds every six minutes. And whether it is

Grace's transforming power, or VNS, the depression is kept at bay.

I'm as realistic about Grace's health challenges as I am about my own. And while I'd love to have her for ten or twelve years, her life span may be considerably shorter. But that realization issues its own kind of challenge—one that makes me strive to make the very most out of every day, every opportunity with a client, every exchange with a student. For now, she's my best gift, and I am hers.

Grace's circle of admirers includes two trainers who saw her potential and worked to correct the limitations imposed by her surgeries. Mark, the second inmate handler of Grace, wrote this tribute to Beth:

"It has been a joy and honor to work with Grace. I know she will fill the hearts of many people with gladness. To have the character and attitude she has, considering all the trauma she's been through, is amazing. Grace is the first dog I've had the privilege of working with and I have been blessed to start with her. Just knowing that these dogs are going to be making it easier for people in need, changing their lives for the better, makes me very proud and happy. I love Grace and I will miss her smile and playful times. Thank you, Beth, for letting me be a part of her life."

And Candi Hitchcock, of NEADS, who intervened in Grace's care and recovery at a crucial time, supplies these reflections:

"Miss Grace NEADS #912 entered our puppy learning center on October 24, 2008. Not long afterward she went on a field trip to a jazz concert with a puppy volunteer. The performer, Wil Darcangelo, picked her up from the crowd and sang "Can't Smile Without You." As time went on, this became her theme song as she began to train to be an assistance dog. She completed her puppy training and was transferred to a prison and placed with an inmate handler.

"The inmates fell in love with her. But the X-ray that all NEADS dogs are required to have in the first year indicated that she had bilateral hip dysplasia and would probably have to be released from the program

due to the diagnosis. We followed the usual protocol and she was to be adopted by a prison staffer who would see the surgeries through and help Grace recover. But a daunting path with some heavy costs lay ahead, and those realities proved more than the potential adopter could manage.

"Although NEADS had never placed a dog with severe health issues I was sure we could find sympathetic humans to donate to her cause. Saint Francis of Assisi, the patron saint of animals, is purported to have said, 'If you have men who will exclude any of God's creatures from the shelter of compassion and pity, you will have men who deal likewise with their fellow men.' It was time to save Grace! Arrangements were made to have her returned to NEADS.

"I knew firsthand what the recovery would be like, having gone through the procedure twice with one of my Goldens, Jake. So Grace would stay with me and my family before and after the surgery. Jake and the other family Golden, Findlay, adored her and kept offering all their toys to her. The orthopedic surgeon who performed the procedure told me something I already knew: 'She is so sweet. All she wants to do is please people.' Choice, not chance, determines destiny. Grace was destined to be special. Donations for Grace were more than enough to pay for her first surgery.

"After a week in the hospital she came home, spending many days outside lying on a sheepskin bed, her shaved rear covered with doggie sunscreen. She needed help walking and makeshift handles were made using a large beach towel as a sling. Finally she was strong enough to continue her recovery and training in the John J. Moran correctional institution. She had her second hip surgery in August and in October, the final surgery on her elbow.

"During this period of time I was able to learn more about Beth and the opportunities she envisioned for Grace in her clinical work with young children and in her classroom psychology classes. As Beth shared stories of this little working dog and how she was changing the lives of many, it became clear to me that they made the perfect team.

"On Saturday, February 26, 2010, a meet and greet was held at the

NEADS campus in Princeton. This get-together celebrates the completed training of a new human/dog team and gives anyone who has had contact with the dog a chance to come and celebrate the success. I was honored to be in the presence of Beth Lewis and her service dog Grace. Grace was happy to see me. However, if Beth left the room she never took her eyes off her. This means my work—the work of the trainers and the NEADS organization—is done. Grace and Beth's work is just beginning."

Chapter Four

My Shadow

Heidi Martin-Coleman and Mercury

It's a day of bright sunshine and high spirits: The town of Easthampton, Massachusetts, is celebrating its founding and residents and friends numbering in the thousands line the main streets to watch a colorful parade unfold. Embedded in the long ribbon of marching bands and historical floats is local resident Heidi Martin-Coleman and her black Lab, Mercury, who wears his distinctive NEADS vest. Heidi and her family have been under assault for the past eight years. First members of her extended family and then, in the past five years, she and her children have been diagnosed with mitochondrial disease, a genetic illness whose symptoms can appear in childhood or later in life and include shortness of breath, generalized muscle weakness and pain, digestive difficulty, and vision and hearing impairments.

But wearing a jaunty red helmet and sailing along in her motorized wheelchair behind a prancing Mercury, Heidi looks far from compromised. She's proud of the work she does with Easthampton's Disabilities Commission, eager to develop more fully her own consulting business, which connects disabled adults and children to useful resources and services, and pressing ahead with the college course work necessary to complete a master's in public health. In fact, it seems entirely appropriate to see Heidi in action, since she is at heart an activist, one who, as she wryly describes it, has "always had a type A personality, even though I now have a type Z body."

Later that day Robert and I have the opportunity to sit down with Heidi and Mercury, whom she affectionately calls "My Shadow." Though she has been deaf for the past three years, her spoken language is perfect and she aims to keep it that way. "Not only do I practice my speech so that I am able to offer disability awareness programs in the schools and accept public speaking engagements, even more crucially

I have to be able to articulate Mercury's commands in crisp and clear ways. Mercury functions as my speech therapist and I practice with him every week."

Heidi begins our conversation by defining the rare disease that has profoundly affected her and her children, mitochondrial disease or "mito" as it's often called.

Even though people with mito are born with the genetic mutation, they can become symptomatic at any time in their lives. The symptoms are extremely variable in type and severity. For me, the first sign of trouble came while I was a student at the University of Massachusetts-Amherst. I had frightening symptoms that were diagnosed as a mild stroke or brain bleed. Over the next twelve years I had intermittent symptoms such as numbness, double vision, muscle spasms, and five years ago, aspiration pneumonia. Stomach tests showed that my GI system didn't function well and from that point on I was fed through a tube in my intestines and a permanent IV line for fluids and medicine.

My youngest daughter, Heather, was born with severe disabilities and special health care needs, and when she was diagnosed with mito, I too had the blood DNA tests and a muscle biopsy. Sure enough, I had mito as well, and had passed the gene to Heather as well as my two older children, Katie and Nick. Tragically, Heather's problems were so severe that she passed away the week before her third birthday. My son has shown some symptoms of mito already, but thus far Katie is asymptomatic.

Every patient is different, even within the same family. In addition to those symptoms I've already described, I also lost my hearing three years ago as a result of strong antibiotics and I have permanent vision problems. Every day begins with a flashing light and a vibrating pillow, and once I am up I have a "mito management" routine that takes about an hour and a half to complete, both morning and night: checks of blood pressure, pulse, temperature, oxygen levels, blood sugar, and preparing special IV fluids and intestinal tube feedings. After the tests I take my medications, and my personal care attendant helps me get washed and dressed. Mercury helps me during this period by fetching shoes and dropped items, putting things in the trash or laundry basket, and most importantly alerting me if something isn't quite right or one of my pumps is misaligned. This last function he performs is amazing, since he can sense a malfunction when even my PCA is unaware of it. If my blood sugar is low or if one of my tubes is a little twisted, prohibiting the full flow of oxygen, Merc will come over and shove his head in my lap. He persists and will not move into a down position, despite my commands. And he's never been wrong; he's never failed to detect trouble—well before I or any other helper realizes anything is amiss. I don't know what this sixth sense is: Does he smell something? Hear something? Does he respond to something in my body language? Whatever it is, it is quite literally a lifesaver for me. It is not something that can be taught, though certainly after I realized what he was telling me, I could praise and reward that behavior.

Given Mercury's centrality to my life, it may sound odd but initially I was skeptical about successfully teaming with a service dog at NEADS.

For one thing, I originally applied for a hearing dog. But after I spoke with several of the staff at NEADS, it became clear that a service dog would be much more useful, given my constellation of needs. I had lots of trepidation when I first met Mercury. Not only did I have multiple needs requiring him to respond to dozens of commands, I had two children at home who would have to accommodate a special working dog into our family life.

Mostly, I think I didn't understand how a human and a dog could become "a team." I hadn't had a dog around since I was a child and no dog I ever experienced could be termed "a partner." My husband and I are a team, a unit tested in ways neither of us would have anticipated. But a canine? Well, the very first day after I met Mercury, I got a glimpse of teamwork. The first morning of Boot Camp is scary because you are schooled in all the things you should never do with a service dog, all the mistakes that impede the progress of a useful working relationship. My head was reeling. Then after lunch we were taken to the big work room upstairs and had to practice the basic commands—heel, down, stay—over and over. Mercury was fine, but I was exhausted. We brought the dogs back to the residential house, had dinner, and retired to our rooms. My PCA went shopping for some supplies we'd need later in the week. So there I was with Mercury. I tried to open my giant duffel bag and the whole thing inverted: everything I'd brought for two weeks in residence went on the floor. I was overwhelmed and dissolved in tears. When I opened my eyes, there was Merc, sitting right beside me with a pair of socks in his mouth. It was as if he said, "Okay, let's take care of this mess. Let's get going." And that was a turning point for me. It dawned on me that he was just as anxious to help me as I was to bond with him. We were on our way.

Of course I had to work my kids and my husband into the team concept as well. I figured there would be hurdles with the kids: Katie is 11 and Nick is 12. Nick has autism; he's high functioning, but he has trouble speaking and I worried that Merc's presence might be problematic for him. Since Nick has Tourette's as well as autism and mito, even though I'm the sole person in the family who can give commands to the dog,

I worried that Nick might "get stuck" on the dog's name—that it would become a verbal tic, and that repetitions of Merc's name could not only be frustrating for Nick, but wholly confusing for Merc. Getting off on the wrong foot here would wound the kids and potentially could be devastating to my fledgling relationship with Merc.

But Mercury's personality helped us there. He's a laid-back guy and doesn't absorb anybody's anxiety, doesn't get hyped up even if others around him are agitated. I decided to write down rules, since Nick is very good with written rules. And both kids mastered them fine, learning in the process some dos and don'ts with service dogs. For example, you can't use Mercury's name just as an endearment because his name is a command. If I say "Mercury," he is instantly at my side. His name means "Come to me," or "Travel with me." (So the kids invented many substitute names for him—some quite creative!) When Mercury is working, he is completely focused on me. He accompanies me everywhere, and while that took a little getting used to, I've come to think of this intelligent, intuitive, black presence as My Shadow, an intrinsic part of me, an extension of who I am.

I think the biggest gift Mercury has given to me is a real and lasting shift in attitude, a regaining of self esteem. For example, before I had him when a person would learn that I was deaf, they would assume I was incapable of communication. If I entered a doctor's office with a PCA or van driver, or even with one of my children, the person at the desk directed questions about me to the person accompanying me. I read lips, I'm fluent in signing, but often I felt invisible, or something inanimate, worthy of only a sideways glance. With Merc by my side I can be alone, an adult seen as being responsible for him and capable of—with some assistance—caring for and speaking for myself.

I suppose in some ways it is as simple—and as deep—as reclaiming my identity. In five years I had plummeted from being an RN, a teacher, a mother, a wife, a musician, a caretaker to being a piece of meat in a wheelchair. All the ways I had defined myself seemed to be nullified. My self-esteem was nonexistent. And yet here I was paired with a dog who had never heard a harsh word in his life, who had never been hit in anger or shamed or abused, who learned all his lessons through positive reinforcement. He was trusting, fresh, and eager to learn new things every day. That's infectious. Quickly, I could see possibilities returning in my life, work I had discarded taken up anew with fresh purpose and some new insights.

My career choices have never been "just a job." I've always made

choices based on my own life experience and on how I thought I could be most useful to people at any given time. When my home life was rather simple and I had lots of free time, I worked with hospice patients, who often needed me to show up early and stay late. When I worked nights with chronic vent patients and taught private trumpet lessons every afternoon, I regularly organized concerts for my patients, bringing my students to perform in hospitals and nursing homes. When my own children were born premature and my son was diagnosed with autism, I became a developmental nurse educator and service coordinator, helping families experiencing similar situations.

Gradually it dawned on me that I could apply to my current circumstances the same working template as I always had used. My decision to work as a disabilities consultant certainly reflects my current situation. Since 2002 I have experienced the birth of a critically ill child and ultimately her death, my own diagnosis with a life-threatening illness, the shift from being the caretaker to being a disabled adult in need of caretakers, and all the attendant social stigmas associated with being disabled. Who could be better positioned to become a disabilities consultant?

People sometimes look at my life, especially in the last five years, and shake their heads, indicating that it has been unrelentingly grim. But although it feels a bit strange to say it, what has been the worst five years of my life has actually provided me with the motivation, the opportunity, and the experience to do the work I have always gravitated toward: helping people with disabilities. Besides, how can your life be grim if you live with a big black Lab who is, at his very core, a huge ham? Merc will do almost anything for a laugh—or more particularly, anything for one of my kids' ice pops: you know, those thin, flavored freeze pops in a plastic tube. Merc adores them and he knows exactly how to clamp his teeth down on the pop, carefully sliding the frozen treat out of the tube. Then he chomps down the ice gleefully, grinning from ear to ear. Sometimes I think Merc knows how to live life better than the rest of us.

When Heidi and Mercury appeared at the spring 2010 graduation ceremony at which Heidi gave the kickoff speech, their presence occasioned huge applause. Heidi's words, leavened with her characteristic honesty and humor, captured the challenges many in the audience were facing:

Five years ago I was given an identity I did not choose. Disabled. Wheelchair bound. Critically ill. Deaf. What happened to my previous identities of mother, nurse, wife, professional? Of course I fought it for a while, but eventually I retreated to the sidelines, becoming Disabled Person.

But then I met Mercury. His self-identity reflected a life lived without fear, anger, hostility, abuse; my identity had been whittled away by illness and disability and society's assumptions about my competence and independence. Each day our bond grew stronger. His trust in me encouraged me to trust myself. Every time he showed me that he respected my authority I regained a little more self-respect.

My identity is changing again. The disabilities remain, but first and foremost I'm again a mother, a wife, a nurse, a professional—and now an advocate, a teacher, a student, and a team member. It is my hope to broaden my online consulting business to become even more effective as an independent consultant for people with disabilities. Mercury and I will help clients establish their own identities by setting goals for employment, self-sufficiency, and independence. My clients may even show up at NEADS some day. You'll know who they are; they'll say Mercury sent them.

Chapter Five

Bred to Serve

Suzanne Goodwin and Berkshire Hills Labradoodles

The road angles sharply to the right and snakes into the colorful foothills of the Berkshire mountains in western Massachusetts. Just past an alpaca farm a striking hand-painted sign announces Berkshire Hills Labradoodles, and the driveway reveals a handsome restored farmhouse dating from the 1700s, now brightly painted in historically accurate tones of terra cotta and bayberry. It is the home of Suzanne (Sunny) Goodwin, artist and breeder of Australian Labradoodles, a canine breed originating about thirty years ago, intentionally bred as an assistance dog.

The breed arose in response to a specific need: a vision-impaired woman in Hawaii requested a guide dog that wouldn't aggravate her husband's severe allergies. Wally Conran of the Royal Guide Dogs in Victoria, Australia, began cross-breeding Labradors and Poodles in hopes of developing an allergy-friendly dog that was also a steady and reliable candidate for guide work. Initially, only a few of the early crosses produced nonshedding and allergy-friendly pups.

In the late 1980s, two breeding and research centers were established in Australia to continue the work Conran began. Rutland Manor and Tegan Park practiced highly selective breedings, producing the current lines of Australian Labradoodles. Australian Labradoodles are consistent in displaying gentle temperaments, are allergy and asthma friendly, do not shed, and display wonderful intelligence. It's not surprising that in addition to their reputation as assistance dogs, they are becoming highly popular as family companions.

When Sunny Goodwin became seriously interested in Australian Labradoodles, she and her daughter flew out to Rutland Manor in Australia. They stayed for three weeks, learning the logistics of selective breeding, whelping several litters of *puppies, and meeting many of the dogs who formed the foundations of Australian Labradoodles in America.*

Such self-starting energy is a pattern in Sunny's life, I learned, as we chatted in the living room of her farmhouse, ringed by fuzzy-faced and beautifully behaved dogs. Her life has had several stops and restarts and she freely admits that she's had to reinvent herself more than once. Willowy of build, with red-blonde hair and a disarming laugh, she doesn't look, at least initially, like someone who could refurbish a derelict farmhouse—stripping the floors, remodeling the kitchen, painting the bedrooms, building a stone facade over an ancient brick fireplace—while caring for a severely disabled house mate, Sandy, her own young child, Zoe, a number of foster children, and an ever-growing collection of Australian Labradoodles. But life has a way of creating its own initiatives, and she's been up to the challenge.

Born into a New Jersey family of six, I was always a huge animal lover. I was especially fond of dogs, but even very early on I was fascinated by reproduction. I frequented the library, scouring the shelves for books about hatching eggs, anatomy, and plant pollination. By the age of ten I had built my own incubator out of some found items in the basement and tried endlessly to hatch chicken and duck eggs. (I came close.) That same year my parents decided to get me my own dog, a Beagle. The memory of receiving Snoopy is indelible for me, and when families with young children come to pick up one of our puppies I try to make the moment as sweet and meaningful for them as it was for me.

I also loved art—design and painting in particular—and that became my original career path. I received a degree in fine arts from the Rhode Island School of Design, moved to New York City, then briefly to New Mexico, then back to the city, where I built a successful business painting murals and wall finishes for the rich and sometimes famous. By then I had my daughter, Zoe, and while we had two cats, dogs weren't really a good idea given my lifestyle at that time.

Then my personal world collapsed: suddenly I found myself a single mother of a three-year-old and facing the need to start over from scratch. Rebuilding my life and Zoe's was a huge challenge and we

did it in incremental steps. My brother and, later, my sister had moved years earlier to the Amherst, Massachusetts, area. I had visited them often, basking in the open spaces, the meadows and mountains, the hiking trails (all calling for a companion dog), and wanted to relocate with Zoe to the area. But how to afford that?

My sister worked in an agency overseeing home shares with folks who were developmentally challenged. She arranged a home share with Sandy, a thirty-five-year-old woman who had suffered a brain aneurysm as a child. Among her many challenges were developmental delays, partial blindness, walking difficulty, seizures, depression, and short term memory loss. Clearly, living with and caring for Sandy were challenges, yet also offered a terrific opportunity for Zoe and me, since I could be a stay-at-home mother for a time and attend not only to Sandy's needs, but to my daughter's and my own healing.

Of course we didn't become a family unit overnight, but gradually, in learning to help one another, we all began to blossom. Sandy works at Riverside Industries, she's become increasingly independent, and now describes herself as "warmhearted, funny, and pretty," words I too would use to describe her. Zoe quickly showed real aptitude in school, gravitating toward literature and languages, and is headed next fall to Mount Holyoke College.

At first, here in the art-rich Pioneer Valley, I was able to really indulge in my art. I exhibited work in several galleries and did lots of teaching of art to children. As rewarding as that was, I began to feel selfish spending time and money on painting when I had my daughter's future, her college expenses in particular, to think about. My passions had to at least pay for themselves. And that's when I turned to my other passion: dogs.

Since my sister and her daughter are both asthmatics and allergic to dogs, I began to do some research on allergy-friendly breeds. When I encountered Australian Labradoodles and the work of Beverley and Angela at Rutland Manor, I was really interested. My sister imported their dog, Reesie, from Australia about eight years ago and once I saw that sweetness, grace, intelligence, and joyful personality on a daily basis, I was completely smitten. My original dog, Willa, arrived from Australia in 2004.

I knew I wanted to begin breeding and needed some space, far more than the cramped quarters I shared with Zoe and Sandy in Northampton would permit. I saw this place in Haydenville online, drove up to see it and, despite its run-down condition and the contractors walking around taking estimates on fixing the roof and shoring up the sills, I called my realtor and said, "This is IT." I could see my dream of Berkshire Hills Labradoodles materializing on this land, in this historic home.

Well, it wasn't that easy. Ten other offers came in on the house, and I quickly realized that most of the other offers would be higher than mine. Forty acres were attached to the property, but they were protected, abutting several neighbors' houses; nobody could build on the land. I certainly didn't need forty acres, so I approached the neighbors, asking if they would like to bid on the property adjacent to their house and add their buying power to mine. And I shared my dream with the sellers, who must have had a fondness for dogs or for folks who still dream dreams and then endeavor to make them happen. Whatever their reasoning, somehow I got this beautiful place, even if it was a huge fixer-upper project. The land is now kept as rolling hayfields, mowed by neighboring farmers who take the hay in exchange for the mowing. It's a peaceful backdrop against which to live and ideal for the dogs. They are never kenneled, and live in the house with many opportunities each day to run free on this scenic land.

Anybody who goes into dog breeding should have the desire to better the breed, to consider the parents' "faults," assets, health, temperaments—and to breed with the intention of producing the most well-balanced, healthy puppy possible. A good breeding program requires a kind of artistry, I discovered, selecting this dog to mate with that dog in order to correct something or produce a quality of coat, or quality of color, or quality of temperament. My childhood love of hatching things and my adult love of designing things come together in Berkshire Hills Labradoodles.

For example, my first dog, Willa, from Australia, brought with her many of the wonderful advantages of a Rutland Manor dog. But her coat was also tightly curled. When I got Kipling, part Australian and part American Labradoodle, his coat was dominant, so the puppies he sired had gentler wavy fleece coats, giving them a softer, sleeker look. Alice's puppies all seem to display her incredibly sweet, laid-back temperament. The vast majority of them go into some kind of therapy work. Paloma, the red daughter of Poppy and Kipling, will produce puppies that have that eye-catching red color, while Mabel produces sweet and solid chocolate brown teddy bears. Consistency of health and temperament are, of course, the primary goals of any responsible breeder. But part of the fun of being a breeder is tweaking your own line according to your own taste and judgment.

Gradually, as I expanded, the dog breeding business became successful and I felt I could extend a helping hand to others. Several foster children became a part of our family for varying periods of time, and the dogs played an integral part in their healing. For example, my foster son Corey, who is a permanent part of our home, has found at the age of eleven both comfort and purpose in living with the dogs, helping care for them, helping me with birthing and training duties. The adult dogs have a wonderfully intuitive sense with children: they love to lie quietly and be hugged or stroked, they play with joyful expressions on their faces, they rarely show anything akin to aggression. They seem to sense when someone is afraid and often a dog would go to a frightened child's bed and simply snuggle in for the night. One of the young girls who stayed here was labeled autistic and she had difficulty making eye contact. She became the constant companion of my loving brown Mabel, who has this habit of looking steadily at "her person" with soft, soulful eyes. Mabel helped that young woman get through some of her darkest times.

The puppies also provided their own built-in lessons, for as they were weaned and matched to homes, and eventually left for their forever homes, I could discuss with the children many of their own experiences with loss, with leaving, and perhaps, with luck, with

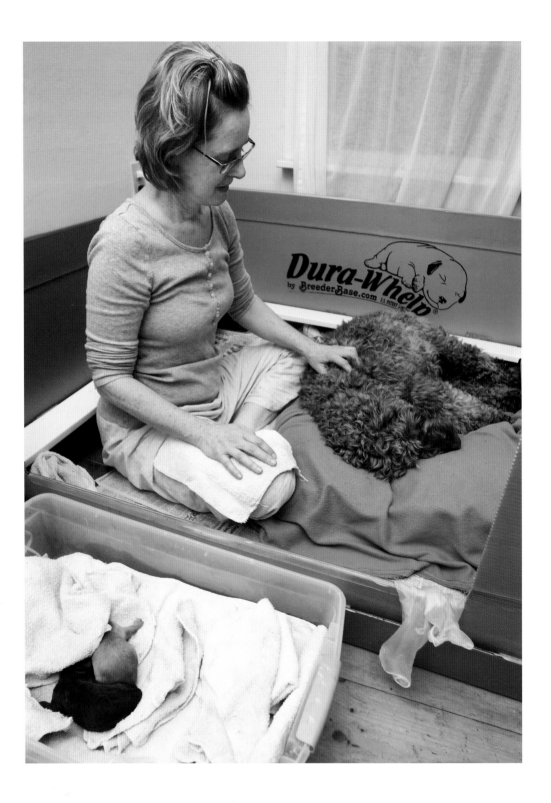

forever homes. [She pauses for a moment, doing some quick mental calculations.] I know at least a dozen of our dogs are currently engaged in doing some sort of therapeutic work and perhaps a dozen more are in training as therapy or service dogs.

Since Labradoodles are still a relatively unknown breed, and since unscrupulous backyard breeders ply their trade with these dogs, as well as with many other breeds, I ask Sunny what misconceptions she'd most like to correct about Australian Labradoodles. She is quick to respond.

They're not a designer dog, a cutesy dog with a silly name who really doesn't have a job. Serious breeders belong to a network of highly organized clubs stressing breed standards, working for the best temperaments and health, striving for breed recognition.

And they aren't an expensive mutt, produced by crossing any old Lab with any old Poodle. (Though I'm sad to say some backyard breeders do exactly that.) As we've discussed, they were bred with a very specific purpose in mind and their history demonstrates highly selective breeding standards: they're strong, they're athletic, they're intuitive.

You know, all breeds evolved out of combinations of other breeds. Other breeds have a breed purpose—chasing rabbits, flushing out pheasant, killing rats, herding sheep. But the majority of us get dogs as family companions. When you think about it, some of the breed "purposes" are actually detriments to being good family companions. Who hasn't allowed a Beagle off a leash to see it put its nose to the ground and disappear over the horizon? Who hasn't experienced an overprotective German Shepherd, or a Border Collie who herds all the school kids standing at the bus stop into a circle? Australian Labradoodles are bred to serve, and if they aren't employed in a specific therapeutic capacity, then their breed purpose is to be the ideal companion. They don't shed, they're allergy friendly, they love everyone, they're very intelligent, they're loyal, and, as Sandy reminds me every day, they get you up, laughing. What could be better than that?

Suddenly, there's a commotion in the back yard. Kipling, the large cream-colored stud dog, is setting up a ruckus and since he's been known to clear the seven- foot fence without even a running start, Sunny hurries out to check. Sure enough, little caramel Carson has found a tiny opening in the fence and has scooted through. "Carson," Sunny yells, "come." And instantly there he is, looking a little sheepish, but hardly crestfallen. I suspect he'll try it again.

Sunny has been considering donating a puppy to NEADS for some time. Although Labs and Golden Retrievers are the most common service dogs in training at the Princeton facility, standard Australian Labradoodles have the sturdiness and intelligence necessary to perform superbly as a service dog; as an added bonus, they, like some Standard Poodles, can be safely placed with clients who suffer from allergies or asthma.

Today, Cindy Lopez and two of her colleagues from the Puppy Training Center at NEADS are arriving to evaluate perhaps a dozen Berkshire Hills Labradoodle pups, to determine if one of them has "the right stuff."

Sunny has gathered the candidate puppies in her "Puppy House," a completely refurbished outbuilding with heat and running water. It is outfitted with two large holding pens and a bright, light-filled exercise room with hardwood floors and plenty of interactive toys. One by one she brings the puppies from the pen into the large room for testing. Each puppy undergoes a sequence of tests designed to reveal which puppies are the most curious, the most bold, the most sociable, the least likely to be distracted. Perhaps the most alarming of the tests involves opening up a large umbrella then dropping it at the feet of the puppy. Some pups shy away, some approach cautiously, and one or two walk right over and climb into the ribs of the upside down umbrella. Mr. Rib-Walker, a big bold chocolate puppy, is chosen as the best possibility.

As Sunny prepares the paperwork, Cindy describes the next months of this puppy's life. In a couple of weeks he'll be transferred to the NEADS Puppy Training Center, where he'll receive some basic training and continued socialization. When he is old enough he'll be transferred to either a private home or the Prison PUP Program, where he'll train in basic obedience for another eight-to-ten months. From there, he'll return to NEADS for his specialized training, his "match," and ultimately the final two-week training with his human partner. When he graduates he'll be about eighteen-to-twenty months old and will be capable of responding to as many as two dozen commands. Cindy assures us that we can follow this puppy through at least the early months of his training and that NEADS will keep Sunny apprised of all of his training progress; she'll be an honored guest at his graduation. It's a pretty thrilling scenario to contemplate, but at the moment the little chocolate guy seems unimpressed, much more interested in chewing on the ribs of the umbrella.

We watch Cindy and her colleagues wind down the road, and Sunny says, reflectively, "It is a thrill to donate a Labradoodle puppy to NEADS, for I know how bright the future will be for that dog and for his or her lucky recipient." And in fact, in a matter of days the Berkshire Hills Labradoodles family, a network of families who own one of Sunny's dogs or aspire to, raise the $1,000 necessary to name the puppy. Little Mr. Rib-Chewer becomes Merlin, a dog hopefully destined to create and spread some magic.

Chapter Six

It's Not a Job; It's My Passion

Dan Ouellette, Christy Bassett, Kathy Foreman

Dan Ouellette

Dan Ouellette cuts an imposing figure: a giant of a man with blond spiked hair and a booming laugh, he moves with the deliberate grace and agility of a professional wrestler—which, as it turns out, he is. He has a quick wit and ready smile and word has it around the halls of NEADS that he is especially effective with kids—that wide range of disabled children who come to NEADS in search of social dogs, or sometimes service or hearing dogs.

Dan lives on the second floor of the residential house where clients stay, paired with their dogs for the first time during their final two weeks of intensive training. His gentle-giant presence is comforting to many nervous residents during this critical bonding and training time, and he often mixes with them as they eat their evening meals, or jokes with the Blue Star Mothers, a support organization of mothers who currently have sons and daughters in the military and who volunteer to prepare special dishes and desserts when a number of veterans are among the clients on campus. He has also trained dogs, been responsible for the kennel facilities, and functioned in a wide range of capacities on the NEADS campus—not an unusual job resume for most full-time staff.

We catch him on the run one bright April Monday morning. He is about to leave for the Hampshire County House of Correction to pick up several inmate-trained dogs, but agrees to sit down for a few minutes to tell his story. "When did you come to NEADS and what interested you about the organization?," I ask, by way of beginning.

"I came here because of community service: a court order." (Broad pause. Big laugh.) *"Just kidding!"*

I sit back and let him roll.

Here's the real story. I knew a person who wanted to get a service dog and who came to NEADS for a match. I came along. I stayed through the training period and I just fell in love with the organization.

At the time I was working in a restaurant and I started volunteering once a week. If you know anything about the restaurant business you know nobody wants to work Saturday nights. I'd say to my boss, "I'll work on Saturday nights if you'll give me Tuesdays off." And then I'd drive the hour here and volunteer from 9 to 4:30 or 5. In a relatively short time a position opened up and I started working initially as a full-time trainer with Kathy Foreman, who guided me through the training of a hearing dog, and subsequently with Brian Jennings, another trainer who guided me through service-dog training. After I completed that training I set out on my own and soon had a couple of strings of dogs I was responsible for training.

As luck would have it, I had the opportunity to work with some of the children with autism who came to be matched with social dogs. That went really well, so the boss said, "No more hearing and service dogs for you: working with children is your special skill and that's what I want you to do." So I started working exclusively with social dogs.

I was still living about an hour from the NEADS campus and it bothered me that, at that time at least, everybody left around 5; nobody stayed behind at the kennel. I quickly realized that it wasn't fair for the dogs to have zero company or exercise in the evenings, so I proposed a tradeoff. I agreed to take care of the kennels in the evening in exchange for living in the second floor apartment of the residential house. Ten years later I'm still living here.

It's good to live in the house with the clients and I believe I'm effective on several levels with them. For one thing, I'm naturally a very social person. I like to talk and I like even better to listen. The two-week intensive training can be taxing for clients. Some of them are struggling because of being away from home and family; others are anxious that they may not be able to bond with the dog or successfully learn the commands that will ensure success. I'm a big guy, a professional wrestler, and I think my presence here at night makes the residents feel safe. Of course I come and go, do my own thing on some nights, but one of my key jobs is to be a calming, consistent presence in the house, helping the clients interact and feel at ease with one another.

"You seem to have mastered a number of jobs over the time you've been here. Is that typical of a staff member at NEADS?," I ask.

I'm not unusual in this respect. Some of us just came up learning several aspects of the work, either by following opportunities as they materialized or pursuing special interests as those interests got sparked. In fact, now we're consciously cross-training people so that staff will have a broad grasp of all the components that make a dog-human partnership work. Even NEADS staff who have what would probably be termed "administrative positions" either know already or are encouraged to learn the basics of dog training and matching. Most administrative staff keep dogs-in-training in their offices during the day to help condition the dogs to "cubicle living" (should their human partner work in an office) and to learn themselves the rudiments of good canine behavior. You've probably noticed as you've walked in and out of offices at NEADS that there's a dog under every desk.

Although the client base in the residential house can at times be quite mixed, we do, when possible, try to group children into shared times, and also group the combat vets. Sometimes the logistics don't work out, but we've found that there are benefits to bringing children together for training at the same time and vets together as a group for their two-week training sessions. It's easy to imagine what those benefits are, if you think about it for a moment. With the military men and women, there's already a built-in camaraderie. They have shared experiences, sometimes things they cannot easily talk about with civilians. When they have a common context, a common language even, bonds are formed much more quickly.

When kids are being trained, we try to work exclusively with them as a group. Almost always the child is accompanied by a parent or family member and there is value in caregivers talking to one another, sharing strategies, as well as kids seeing other kids who are also attempting to overcome obstacles. We try to create conditions that are optimal for our clients: we want them to learn as much as they can in their two weeks with us and be as comfortable as possible in the process.

In my special work with the kids I find that I'm often stumbling upon new ways to help simply by doing the work. We've had kids sleep through the night for the first time ever, kids who talk for the first time ever, kids who say "I love you" for the first time ever. We want to figure out exactly what is making that happen and then maximize it. I've had several moments I'll never forget, but one really stands out. A child, one who was completely nonverbal, was matched with a black Lab named Pride. When I spoke with his mom before they came for training, I told her who the dog would be and what the name would be. I added "You want to begin to start teaching your son the dog's name." Well, she was incredulous, and she insisted, fiercely, that her son did not and would not speak. She was wholly frustrated with me.

I could understand her frustration, but I then asked, "Does he make any noises at all? Grunts, groans, squeaks?" "Yes," she said quickly. "Well, if we teach him to make whatever sound he makes and then give the dog a cookie, the dog will soon learn to come when the boy makes that sound. That sound will become Pride's name."

By the time he came for training the boy could mouth the word Pride, but he couldn't say it aloud. But by the end of training, when I would say to him, "What's your dog's name?," he would say out loud, "Pride, Pride, Pride." When graduation rolled around the mother, son, and dog went up on stage. The mother gave the thank-you speech, then held the microphone to her son's lips. We all held our collective breath. "What's your dog's name?," she asked.

Loud and clear: "PRIDE."

You know, I have no special training with children, but I find kids on the autism spectrum intriguing. In those moments when you can see the gears working, I want so much to find a way to reach them and help them bond with a dog who will become a best friend. It's like they present a whole bunch of doors and the challenge is figuring out which one is going to open to let me in. The strategies I devise don't always work, but when they do, well, that's all the reward I need.

Dan stands up and Robert and I wave him on, knowing he has a date with some eager young dogs. Halfway out the door he pivots and calls out to Robert. "Do you like wrestling? If you want to see a match I'll send you tickets. I wrestle under the name Freight Train."

And out the door he chugs.

Christy Bassett

Christy Bassett is, along with two other trainers and an apprentice trainer, responsible for the vigorous and diverse training of assistance dogs at NEADS. Energetic and youthful, with long dark brown hair, Christy and her legendary training skills often surface in conversations with clients. Since arriving at NEADS in 2002, Christy has trained the full range of assistance dogs who graduate from the NEADS program. She's also worked with inmates who are training pups in the Prison PUP Program. She understands intimately what is involved in producing a superb assistance dog and she'd be the first to endorse the service dog trainer's mantra: "Love, patience, repetition." Or as she and Brian Jennings, senior trainer, sometimes put it: "Patience, patience, patience."

I went to college at the University of New England in Biddeford, Maine, to get my degree in psychology and animal studies. Taken together, these two fields of study created a curriculum in animal behavior. Although I've always loved animals and knew I wanted to work with them in some capacity, I wasn't attracted to veterinarian school or to working as a groomer, researcher, or shelter worker. I wanted a more personal relationship with the animals than these jobs implied, so I focused on training. At first I was drawn to the exotic appeal of marine animals. But getting a job at Sea World was a long shot and I've never been a strong swimmer. I also looked at Guide Dogs for the Blind, though there weren't many facilities in the New England area and the competition was fierce.

As my college years were coming to an end, I realized that I needed to complete an internship in the field I wanted to pursue. It was during my search for possible internships that I found NEADS. I was accepted into the six-week instructor training in the summer of 2002. After completing that course I returned to college to finish my senior year. Throughout that year I maintained contact with Executive Director Sheila O'Brien and Senior Trainer Brian Jennings, and made trips down to volunteer whenever I could. Close to graduation time I sent a formal job request to NEADS, but they weren't hiring immediately. Sheila O'Brien assured me, however, that she would help me make contact with other organizations in the assistance dog world and she reminded me that hiring needs often change suddenly, with openings popping up at any time. One week later Sheila contacted me saying that the board had approved a position for me as a trainer's apprentice. I came,

absolutely loved the work, and can't imagine doing anything else.

Now, as an advanced trainer, I work with all types of dogs and clients. We train hearing dogs, service dogs, walker/balance dogs, social dogs, and therapy dogs. We currently have three advanced trainers and one instructor trainer, and among us we divide the work that comes through the program at any given time. We each have a string of dogs secured either from our puppy program or from animal shelters, and during advanced training we evaluate them to decide what careers they are best suited to.

During my first year at NEADS I was a trainer's apprentice under the tutelage of Brian Jennings. I learned the ropes of dog selection, training, and matching, as well as how to work with clients and problem solve after the team has gone home. When you think about it, service dogs not only have to master a repertoire of skills, they must also display an absolutely consistent temperament. They need to be calm and friendly, not fearful, anxious, or, especially, not aggressive. They need to accept strangers, children, other animals and they need to be comfortable with wheelchairs, canes, crutches, and various assistive devices. But they also have to be unobtrusive to the public so that they can blend into any setting without calling special attention to themselves: a classroom, a public bus or train, a restaurant, a conference room. A crucial part of our training hinges on developing the natural personalities of the dogs to ensure reliable responses, even in new situations. That reliability is at least as important, perhaps more important, than teaching a dog to perform a set of tasks on command.

After I completed the apprentice year of training I was promoted to advanced trainer with my own string of dogs. Currently at NEADS, advanced trainers not only work with dogs in the kennel in advanced training, but they are also in charge of at least one prison program. That means that we work with puppies who have come from our own puppy learning center and who are placed with inmates for approximately a year's training. Most recently we've added a Halter Dog program for autistic children and a Trauma Alert Dog program for veterans with Post Traumatic Stress Disorder. These programs are still in the trial phase. But coupled with the Canines for Combat Vets program, these programs indicate some new directions for NEADS in the coming years.

As technology changes, so do our training styles and the needs of our clientele. Deaf people now have the use of many assistive devices that can help them in ways never before thought possible. Amputees now have better and more advanced prosthetic limbs that simulate the way real joints and sensations work. Wheelchair users now have access to chairs that can stand them straight up and that can climb stairs. But with all of these advances, nothing can take the place of a dog. Animals can think, can figure things out, and, best of all, can love you back—something that no machine can do. Assistance dogs will always be needed. We'll just need to expand our perspectives and explore new ways they can help people.

I see startling and heartwarming changes in clients' lives after they are matched with their dogs. I have one client who often pops into my mind, a young woman, twenty-one and using a manual wheelchair when I first met her. She lived with her parents when she first applied for a service dog, and when she came to training she was extremely shy. She asked her mother to do everything for her, including ordering food at a restaurant or talking to strangers in public. Over the course of the two-week training period, she began to open up. Her dog gave her more confidence and that translated into greater independence. By the time she took her certification test at the end of training she was confidently pushing herself through the mall, smiling at her dog, asking him to hand money and take change from cashiers, and not even looking back reflexively at her mother.

Although I had often used the line "Dogs help people to become more independent," this client dramatically illustrated that truth. I kept in touch with her over the years and she relayed to me that when she got a new job working with children, she moved out of her parents' home. Living independently in a mobile home, she often had to advocate for her right to bring her dog into public places. She also confided that her father had often been unkind to her and one of the reasons she chose to leave that house was that her dog sensed the hostility and tried to intervene.

Recently her dog became ill and she could no longer afford to take care of him. She took out loans to cover the ever-increasing cost of his care, but gradually it became clear that he would have to retire. It was emotionally wrenching to meet with her to discuss this reality. But she had changed from a girl into a woman. She had made sacrifices to keep her beloved dog as long as she could. And although the dog had to be retired, she maintained a positive attitude, giving all the credit for how far she had come to her dog. "Look at me," she said. "I took a public bus to Boston, changed lines, and ended up in Worcester, hundreds of miles from home. I never could have done that without him." She called just the other day to say that her church had started a fund to raise money for a new service dog for her. Currently they have about $1,000 in that account. I think of Josie whenever I am about to match a dog with a client. I ask myself, "Is this the dog that can bring out the best in this person, can complement their weaknesses, best address their needs?" If so, then I get a special feeling, knowing that when I match this dog with this partner, neither of their lives will ever be the same again.

Kathy Foreman

Kathy Foreman, the client coordinator at NEADS, holds the crucial responsibility of creating a client profile that is used to match a client with the best assistance dog. The process is a meticulous one, hinging on a discerning knowledge of the client and his or her needs, a thorough understanding of the dog's training and temperament, and a thirty-year history of working in almost every capacity in NEADS. Kathy has the "big picture" of the NEADS mission in her head, undergirded by hands-on experience in most of its programs. It's a heavy load of experience and history to balance on the shoulders of a petite, curly-haired woman with a lilting laugh. But as she insists with some regularity, "NEADS is my passion. It's not a job; it's a passion."

Since so much rides on the "match" between client and assistance dog, I ask Kathy if she'll break down the components of the process.

Well, certainly the interview process is the first component and the steps I take in that process I've refined over the years. Initially, I spend literally hours on the phone with potential clients who are wondering if they qualify for a dog, if they really want a dog, if their disability will make it difficult, maybe even impossible, for the dog to get enough exercise. We're interested in making the best matches we can—ones that enhance the lives of the clients but also protect the needs of our dogs, so sometimes I have to ask the hard questions.

We begin with a written application (also available online) that explores questions of lifestyle, most particularly why a person wants a dog; I review that, noting any red flags that may appear. An applicant might say, for example, "I need a dog for protection," and I'll know that isn't a part of our mission.

The next step is to set up an interview here. (We can also send them a video format if they're unable to get to our campus.) They need to supply their medical history. And then I meet with each candidate one-on-one for perhaps an hour and a half or two hours of conversation. While they're here I have them meet a few dogs, just to see how they handle the dogs or react to dogs in general.

Since I trained dogs for the first fifteen years of my time at NEADS I learn the temperaments of the types of assistance dogs as well. I generate a profile of each candidate that the trainers and I match with the available dogs. We consider a number of things as we discuss the match: the physical needs of the client in relation to the dog's height, weight, and strength, the personality of the client and the temperament of the dog, the support system that exists for the client, whether the client works and, if so, what the circumstances of the workplace will be for the dog. Of course I can't ensure success 100 percent of the time, but over the years I've gathered enough experience to help anticipate the pitfalls and, with luck, avoid making mistakes. One of the best compliments I can receive is when, after meeting a client for the first time and working with him or her and the dog for a day, a trainer says, "We've made a very good match here."

As you may have heard clients mention, we're here for them after

they leave the facility, after they graduate. If a client has a training question, they can call our trainers, Christy, Brian, or Erin. If it's an adjustment problem—say they're concerned about public access—then they call me. I'm pretty sure I'm viewed, after all these years, as a "mother," and I'm perfectly willing to try to sort out the difficulty, suggest ways to solve it, what staff member to contact, or simply offer support. Probably the hardest calls for me to field come when someone has had a dog for many years and death claims the dog. They call and sob. And I cry too. Somebody has to listen, to help absorb the enormity of that loss. NEADS wants to help with the whole process and, as we all know, death is an integral part of that process.

Being a good interviewer is, I think, mostly about being a good listener—and an interactive listener. I always keep in mind when talking with a client, "This could be my mother, my sister, my son," and I want to give them exactly the quality of attention I would wish for my loved ones. I want them to be unafraid to ask questions that are perhaps uncomfortable. I want to help them understand that their partner is a dog, not a robot. Or that their canine partner isn't a human mind wearing a furry body. I'm here to help them understand what they need to bring to the team. It can't just be about, "What can this dog do for me?" It's about partnership.

So I remind them that their dog will need twenty to thirty minutes of aerobic exercise each day, each and every day. Without that exercise, the dog's energy gets pent up and can come out in destructive ways. So the client has to find an enclosed area where the dog can be safe off-leash to run and chase a ball or a Frisbee each and every day. I have to keep going back to these hard questions: Do you have the energy? Do you have the commitment? It's essential to face those questions right up front, before any emotional investment in the dog is made.

I also want to discover in an interview if the client is a good problem solver. Nothing remains constant in life, so it stands to reason that some things will change during the lifetime of this match. Perhaps the client's health will decline over the course of the team's work together. And we're realizing now, especially with our clients who are returning vets, it's quite possible that some of their health and mobility issues will improve as they get more proficient with their prostheses or as technology improves whatever equipment they use.

Beyond the immediate and specific needs of individual teams, I think a number of us at NEADS feel the pressure to expand, since the need for assistance dogs has expanded—some might say explosively—in the last decade. If you need to grow, in what direction? Certainly those new directions are topics at every board of directors meeting these days.

Clearly we sense the urgency of the PTSD program as it figures in our future. I get some heartbreaking emails from returning vets who suffer debilitating symptoms with PTSD. One recent one said, "I've become a stranger to my wife and my children don't recognize me. I'm writing to you as my one last Hail Mary pass—to see if you can give me back the life I had." That's dramatic—and a dog may not be the answer, but it grabs at your heart. It makes me want to think about the needs that are out there, how to weigh them, how to respond with purpose and commitment.

It's hard to estimate if and when the U.S. Department of Veterans Affairs and the federal government will get on board to support programs like placing trauma/alert dogs with returning vets suffering from PTSD. Huge agencies like to work with numbers, and programs such as ours like to work with individuals. Sometimes we don't succeed and a dog is returned. Sometimes a dog makes a measurable difference in a person's life. And sometimes a dog makes a spectacular difference. We can't really quantify our results, but rather we look at results on a case-by-case basis. I don't think we'll ever lose our emphasis on an individual life and an individual dog.

You know that old story about all the starfish thrown up on a beach after a violent storm? Two companions walk by and one bends over, picks up a starfish and throws it back into the sea. His companion scoffs, "picking up one doesn't make any difference." His companion replies, "Well, it made a difference to that starfish."

I think our emphasis will always be on making a difference for each and every team we send out into the world. Perhaps I'm especially touched when the vets come to our campus, for my son is a former Marine. These returning soldiers are coming from all over the country and they have no idea what to expect. It's a leap of faith for them. I go over to the house and greet them, talk to them, maybe take them to supper. Sometimes when they say goodbye I'll whisper, "Tell your mother she did a good job." And they'll smile and nod and give me a hug.

As I look back on my thirty years at NEADS I realize I've met many wonderful people, crossed paths with people I'd otherwise have missed knowing in such deep and gratifying ways. But I'd also have to say that some of my fondest memories circle around the dogs I've saved. At the very beginning of NEADS, when it was the Hearing Ear Dog Program, Sheila and I were finding all the dogs, doing all the dog training, training the human partners, giving speeches and raising money—often just the two of us—and we used only shelter dogs. This was before spay and neuter programs really got off the ground and the shelters in the Northeast were almost all kill shelters. This may be an odd thing to single out, but when I think about accomplishments, I think about all the dogs we saved. Sometimes we'd walk into a shelter and twenty-five dogs were available, twenty of which wouldn't last the week. We took dozens and dozens of dogs that were throw-outs, some literally hours away from being put down, who after rescue and training became vitally useful and much-loved hearing dogs. We also rescued some dogs we knew wouldn't likely make the grade as hearing dogs, but were loving and we knew we could find good homes for them.

The universe is energy, I believe, and when you live your life you either add positive energy or negative energy. I hope I've added positive energy. And I have no intention of stopping.

Chapter Seven

Raising Awareness

Alexis Courneen and Sooner

Meeting Alexis Courneen, her husband, Jason, their two daughters, Brynna, six, and Riley, four, and their big bold Lab Sooner is like walking into a Hallmark card. For one thing, they are all as blond as champagne-colored Sooner. For another, their house is alive with the sounds of laughter, of friendly toy-possession tussles among not only Sooner and Tyson, a chocolate Lab mix, but also Ginger, a tiny rescued Chihuahua, who doesn't seem to realize she weighs five pounds. But this is a family that has already met more challenges than most of us do in a lifetime; they know some additional hurdles lie ahead.

Alexis, who describes herself as a self-starter, accelerated her pace through high school, graduating at seventeen, ready to be on her own and work her way through college. She realized that joining the military would help pay for her college expenses and since there was a military tradition in her family, she joined the Coast Guard. "I didn't want to duplicate the path other family members had taken and since people in my family had joined the Army, Navy, Air Force, and Marines, I decided on the Coast Guard."

She was stationed in the Staten Island area, patrolling New York Harbor. One day while on patrol Alexis and another crew member were seriously injured; she suffered blunt force trauma to her right arm, neck, head, and back.

We were slammed into a metal buoy that we had craned on our boat. The initial impact crushed all the nerves in my right arm as well as damaging four cervical discs in my neck. I had surgery to rebuild a channel for the nerves in my right elbow. But the day after I got my cast off from the surgery I was invited for a morale day on the USS Intrepid. I slipped in the rain and fractured my pelvis. I developed arthritis in

my right arm, neck, shoulder, and both hips. But it was really a year or two ago that I began to get progressively sicker. I have an autoimmune disease, though just which one has yet to be determined.

The good news is that the VA is taking responsibility for some of what is happening to me, but the bad news is they aren't figuring it out with any speed or accuracy. My medical expenses are covered, but we don't appear to have very good detectives on my case. Perhaps it's because traditionally the VA system hasn't seen many women, particularly many young women: I just turned thirty-one. Fortunately, that's beginning to change. With the arrival of female combat casualties from Iraq and Afghanistan they're beginning to establish women's clinics and are trying to be more attentive to the needs of women and the injuries and diseases women are more prone to get.

My initial injuries and surgeries occurred in 1999, 2000, and after 2001, when we had private insurance. I did all my medical work around the pregnancies privately. It became apparent, however, that my existing medical problems created real risk factors for pregnancy. We have two beautiful daughters, and when I learned it would be too dangerous to my heart to continue, we said, "Enough. We're thankful for who we have."

I learned of NEADS in an indirect way. Jason and I, growing up in Newington, Connecticut, were accustomed to seeing the Fidelco dogs, seeing eye dogs, training in malls and public parks in Newington and Wethersfield. But when we moved into this house we lived right across the street from the most amazing family. They have twins, one of whom is autistic and the other has a range of physical disabilities. The twins are almost ten years old now and we watched their parents go through their search for aids of one kind or another to make life easier for the boys. They had a close friend in their autism community who had gotten a service dog for their autistic child. So we were introduced to at least the idea of service dogs, dogs not trained exclusively for the blind, in that way.

Riley, our younger daughter, was about to head to preschool. And it suddenly dawned on me that I wouldn't have somebody around to call Jason if I fell. I'd be here alone every school day. I discussed this with my doctor and she advised me to come up with a solution to ensure my own safety. She said, quite pointedly, "You need to either go to a day care center during weekdays or find some kind of home help."

I had already spent a lot of time hanging out at the VA, a place where I'm always the youngest, and I told myself, "Well, you may not be completely self-sufficient, but surely there are ways you can be safe and still retain some independence."

I found NEADS on the Internet and spoke to the folks in the office that very day. It was a hard step to take. I knew that if I got a dog I'd have to come clean to lots of folks who didn't know the extent of my disability. But I saw NEADS had a program particularly for vets, and despite my caution, we arranged for an interview with Kathy Foreman.

Kathy is amazing. She did the intake interview and she has the gift of creating comfort and candor in that otherwise nerve-jangling setting. Since she used to be a dog trainer, she also is up to date on the personalities of the dogs in training and as she assesses the needs of the client and the personalities of the dogs, she, together with others at NEADS, makes wonderful matches. We came away from that interview both comforted and excited. Kathy told us about their Canines for Combat Veterans program, where, if you qualify, NEADS fully funds the service dog. They work with organizations like the Delta Society (who helped with Sooner), or with a funding organization called the Tower of Hope. The Tower of Hope is an organization Cathy Carilli and her second husband, Mark, founded to honor the memory of her first husband, Tom Sinton, lost in the Twin Towers' collapse on September 11, 2001. As the months passed and people coped with their loss and grief, Cathy and Mark felt that their animals helped them get through the tragedy. And since Iraq and Afghanistan combat vets were starting to stream back home not too long after 9/11, they decided to focus their funding efforts primarily on vets. Even though it was the Delta Society that sponsored Sooner, along with several smaller sponsors like the New England Arts for Animals, I want to endorse the vital work done by all of these organizations. Service dogs are very expensive and those organizations that help to defray some of the expense for a client are godsends. Sooner has given me the gift of independence. I can't imagine life without him. So I want to continue to support sponsoring organizations in any way I can.

Well, the day came when Kathy called and said, "We have a match for you and he's called Sooner. We'll put together a constellation of sponsors and we'll make it work for you financially."

As thrilled as we were, I was still more than a little unsure. After all, it involved two weeks away. Jason could come with me for only three days and once the dog was living with me, we were "on our own." I feared I would have an episode and not be able to get out of bed. I couldn't imagine being away from my two very young daughters for two weeks, even though my mother had volunteered to be with them when Jason was at work. But Kathy has a way of saying "It will all work out" in a voice that is very convincing.

And so I went to meet Sooner. I knew he was a yellow Lab, but I hadn't seen a picture. And when he was brought into the room I just sobbed. We bonded immediately. He looked just like "family" and he seemed to sense he was, even from the first.

Whatever the reason, Sooner and I were meant for each other, and that was evident from Day 1. In fact, I grew very emotional when he couldn't accompany back to "the house" the first night. Luckily, I had Jason with me.

After I had been there several days I got a call that made me realize how crucial it was for me to come home with Sooner. My mother called, saying that my older daughter, Brynna, wanted to talk with me, but that

she might be hard to understand since she was a little overwhelmed. I listened, trying to encourage her to talk. She was sobbing. And she said: "Mommy, Mommy, I miss you so much. But I'm glad you met Sooner and that he is going to come home with you, because now, when I go to school I know you'll be safe."

That is a story I couldn't tell for a long time without sobbing myself. I hadn't realized what a weight she was carrying on her little shoulders every time she went off to school.

As I trained with Sooner I began to realize all the ways in which he could help me. Not only can he fetch things, perhaps most importantly my phone, he can also help with my balance. Increasingly, I experience balance issues or weakness in my legs that results in difficulty going up and down stairs and sometimes just, unexpectedly, falling. I had trained my old Lab mix, Tyson, to walk beside me on the stairs, but Tyson has his own bad arthritis now and he was none too steady on the stairs himself. Sooner positions himself in tight on one side and I touch the wall on the other, and that's pretty secure. If I fall, he comes and stands in front of me, braces himself, and I can use him like the seat of a chair, to steady myself into a standing position. If I fall and can't get up, or get hurt, he brings my phone so that I can call Jason.

But perhaps most miraculously, he can sense when I'm about to have "an episode," a migraine or that kind of paralytic fatigue I was describing earlier: it feels like your battery is registering zero. I don't know if he smells a scent of some sort (like a seizure dog does) or reads my body language in a particular way, but Jason knows when Sooner comes over and stands right beside me, or, if I'm on the couch, jumps up and lies right on my lap, an episode is coming. If Sooner senses I'm in trouble, he won't leave my side.

At first that bothered me some, since it's such a clear signal. I'm a private person and I'm not prone to talking about my health issues endlessly. Of course people know I've had multiple surgeries. You can't hide a twelve-inch scar on your arm. But I haven't shared many details of the complications that followed. Even some members of my family didn't know the extent of my disability. I was brought up to believe that you powered through your difficulties, not offering any excuses. And so I think I hid some of my health problems from friends and family, probably becoming more isolated in the process.

With Sooner, everything was out in the open. When you take a service dog into a public space, it's clear you need him. And when Sooner grows super-protective of me, I realize—as does anybody I'm with—that I'm even more vulnerable than usual.

But I think Sooner's presence forced me to be open about my disability and that openness was the source of healing for us all. Brynna and Riley's friends thought their mom was cool because she had this beautiful dog that could do so many things on command. So that was their opening to talk to their peers about what had happened to me.

Sooner is wonderful with all kids, but I noticed something quite interesting at the bus stop. The school bus stops right in front of our house, where both the across-the-street twins and our kids all attend a school for, among others, hearing-impaired kids. The twin who has autism came straight over to Sooner and started to interact with him.

This happens every morning, and seeing the advantages, now our neighbors are looking into applying for a service dog for him. Sooner is a center from which many circles widen, so that his presence benefits more people than just me or my immediate family. I think, for example, it's enriching for our girls to see a wide range of disabilities; that's one of the reasons we like them to attend a school where many students are hearing impaired. Just as they have learned to do many things for themselves (that four- and six-year-olds typically have their mothers do), they're growing up with a wider and richer understanding of how some people have to navigate this life. I wish this special kind of awareness and understanding touched more people.

In fact, Jason and I were talking about this the other day, speculating that hiding disabilities, or categorizing a wide range of disabilities under one label—blind—may be a generational thing, an attitude that is passing. It used to be when any of us saw a person with an assistance dog the automatic assumption was that the person was blind. That's changing. The other day we were in the supermarket with Sooner and we overheard a conversation between a mother and her teenage son. The mother said, "Oh, look there's a seeing eye dog." Her son, noticing that I was not blind, said, "No, Mom, that's a service dog."

I started out from high school full of a sense of purpose, self-sufficient, and determined to achieve my goals. But injuries changed those carefully constructed plans. I find, with the help of my family and Sooner, I am recovering a purpose in my life. I speak at as many fundraising events for service dogs as I can. I see as my purpose making people more and more aware of the invaluable help a service dog provides. It has made all the difference in my life. Raising awareness: that's my mission.

Changing Needs at NEADS

Canines for Combat Vets and the Prison PUP Program

Sheila O'Brien

Sheila O'Brien came to work at NEADS in 1978, shortly after graduating from college, joining the fledgling organization when its sole mission was the training of hearing dogs. In the next twenty-five years as NEADS grew, Sheila worked in virtually all training, matching, developmental, and fundraising capacities, assuming the position of executive director in 1984 and CEO in 2009, before leaving to assume a position as director of external relations at America's VetDogs in Smithtown, New York. Hers was the shaping hand in widening the mission of the organization to include social and therapy dogs, ministry dogs, service dogs, and trauma alert dogs. She was particularly instrumental in developing the Canines for Combat Veterans program at NEADS and the Prison PUP Program, which accelerated an assistance dog's training by utilizing the time and skills of inmate dog trainers. I ask her about the evolution of these two distinctive programs.

NEADS first developed a combat vets program in 2005 when it became apparent that returning veterans from the Iraq/Afghanistan wars were coming home with a different set of needs than in previous wars. Most of them were young (average age twenty-five), strong, and athletic, but had suffered amputations, head wounds, memory loss, and PTSD. I followed the demographics of the disabled population in our country and I could see that these wounded warriors from Iraq and Afghanistan differed significantly from the clientele NEADS had served in the past. Most of our previous clients were in their thirties and forties and needed assistance dogs to help them cope with a progressive disease or disability, like MS or a progressive hearing loss. While this population will always be central to our mission at NEADS, we quickly realized after visiting Walter Reed Army Medical Center that this young disabled population was unlike any we had ever known. They spend a long time recovering from their wounds, many hospitalized for twenty-four to thirty months. And when they've recovered, they don't want wheelchairs and crutches, they want dogs.

The increase in our Prison PUP Program was one response to the exploding number of returning combat veterans. Although the Prison PUP Program dates from 1998, well before the great influx of returning vets, we expanded it rapidly to accommodate this sudden need.

In the '90s our procedure was to house our puppies with foster families as they completed their early training. Not only was it difficult to find enough foster homes, the progress on the training was pretty slow. Foster families don't have time to devote to puppy training each and every day; often weekends were the only times available for training sessions. When the puppies returned to our home facility, they had only rudimentary skills and often had to spend another six months in training. Clearly, we needed effective and more plentiful puppy trainers. At the same time I was approached by Michael Maloney, the then-commissioner of Correctional Facilities in Massachusetts, who wanted to start a prison pup program. Such programs were in their infancy then and Commissioner Malone argued that qualified inmates wanted and needed an effective and safe way to give back to the society they had violated. A Prison PUP Program fit the bill.

At first I was skeptical, or at least worried—hesitant about placing our precious puppies behind bars. But I began hearing about other experiments placing dogs in medium- and low-security prisons and I thought it was worth a try. Two days before Christmas in 1998, with the encouragement of Lynn Bissonnette, at that time superintendent at North Central Correctional Institution in Gardner, Massachusetts, we placed two puppies, Pax ("peace") and Zenus ("gift from God"), in the

Gardner facility. What was a tentative experiment rapidly became a win-win situation for us all.

The inmates had plenty of time on their hands—and they could use that time productively, training the puppies. We learned to send our senior trainers to teach the inmates how to work most effectively with their dogs and the puppies left the prison setting on weekends to be socialized by weekend puppy raisers. This coordinated effort cut the training time in half. We could provide more dogs much more rapidly to our waiting clients and the inmates could "give back" in ways they knew were very meaningful. The success of the program was its own best advertisement: NEADS now has Prison PUP Programs in thirteen correctional institutions in Massachusetts, Rhode Island, Vermont, and Connecticut, and about 90 percent of our dogs are trained through the prison system. Now there are more than forty prison pup programs across the United States, and they are being introduced to other countries. It is one of the great success stories in the world of assistance dogs.

To explore the workings of this well-coordinated effort, I spoke with combat veteran Kevin Lambert, who is paired with Ronnie, one of the first trauma alert dogs to graduate from the NEADS program; with Jacob ("Jake") Liptak, who trained Ronnie at the Hampshire County House of Correction; and with Heather Dawson, who was one of Ronnie's weekend puppy raisers. Their interlocking stories demonstrate the power of the program and the benefits to each participant.

Kevin Lambert and Ronnie

Since Kevin Lambert returned from a sixteen-month Army deployment in Iraq and recovered from a severe spinal injury and PTSD, he has been employed by the state of Massachusetts as an outreach coordinator for SAVE, Statewide Advocacy for Veterans' Empowerment. Although he lives in Haverhill in the northeastern part of the state, his work takes him all over the Commonwealth and he arranged to meet us at one of his satellite offices. Although he is not one to dramatize his military service, he was a member of the 172nd Stryker Combat Brigade, based in Fairbanks, Alaska, whose infamous 450-plus day Iraq tour of duty was one of the longest combat deployments of any Army unit since Viet Nam. Kevin is also one of the first recipients of a trauma alert dog from NEADS and a member of the initial pilot program studying the interactions and supports that assistance dogs can provide for soldiers who have experienced and may still be grappling with PTSD. Clearly, he's a high-energy guy. He speaks rapidly and with conviction. In fact, one of his favorite words is "Absolutely!"—said with emphasis, in a deep baritone voice. Ronnie, a handsome, athletic black Lab, accompanies Kevin everywhere; her eyes rarely leave his face.

Nobody in my family encouraged me to choose the military, but it was something I always knew I wanted to do. I grew up in Dracut, Massachusetts, and would have enlisted right out of high school. But since I had been injured as a kid in a car accident, losing my spleen and suffering a mild brain injury, I had to wait a bit to get medical clearance. We always had dogs in our home, so I didn't have to learn to love dogs. But then Ronnie is far from a pet. She is a highly trained assistant, a crucial tool in the work that I do, not to mention a constant support and comfort for me.

I was assigned to the 172nd Stryker Combat Brigade out of Fairbanks, Alaska, and we were deployed in Iraq from August 2005 to December 2006. We had successfully completed our one-year deployment in Mosul when, just twelve hours before we were to leave to go home, [Secretary of Defense Donald] Rumsfeld announced "the surge." Experienced troops were needed and so our homecoming was canceled and we were sent to Bagdad for the next four months. That was an interesting turn of events.

I was a light machine gunner for the infantry. Occasionally I went out in an armored vehicle, but mostly I went on sniper patrols, on foot, carrying my weapon and all my gear. Eventually I broke two bones in my spine, probably because of the weight I was carrying. It

went unrecognized for some time and as a result I suffered extensive nerve damage. Doctors later surmised that the swelling kept the bones in place and so I could keep functioning. But once I got home and the swelling went down I knew I had trouble. I could barely walk and when I did try, I was bent to one side. I saw a spine surgeon and a knee surgeon at Massachusetts General Hospital, received a number of spinal injections, and eventually learned to live with a chronic pain disorder. I don't like to take lots of medications since they don't really address the problem, they simply mask it. I take only the pills I absolutely have to in order to function.

After my discharge from the Army in December of 2007, I went to work for SAVE. At first my work centered on suicide prevention. Because I myself had experience with PTSD and knew the stigma it could carry, I think I could do a more effective intervention with a veteran who was experiencing a crisis—simply by talking, sharing experiences, trying to open the door to treatment possibilities.

More recently SAVE has been emphasizing education, treatment, and support for not only veterans but also their families. The transition from a combat zone back into civilian life impacts the entire family. So although I still do one-on-one interventions, my job focus has shifted a bit: I've been looking at some resources that can help the whole family, working to connect people at risk with those supports and benefits that can make a real difference. More specifically, I'm working with the Department of Higher Education to help veterans who could benefit from going back to school. It's one thing to know that you can access the GI Bill, but it's something else to figure out which schools might be most receptive to and supportive of returning vets seeking to further their education. I'm also working with what is called the Jail Diversion Program, exploring the best ways to keep vets from landing in jail with DUIs. And I've been working with the Homeless Vets Program, trying to connect this discouragingly large population with affordable housing. All three of these fields seek to stabilize the lives of returning veterans, but also, by extension, to stabilize the lives of those family members who love and care for them.

It was, in fact, through my job as a coordinator of services for returning vets that I discovered NEADS' Canines for Combat Vets program. About three years ago I went out to tour the facility and learn about their services. I was very impressed and initially we had some conversations about placing a walker dog with me. But I could manage reasonably well physically; my more pressing needs, both personally and professionally, revolved around psychological and emotional support.

Trauma alert dogs are special in the ways in which they can be used therapeutically. Each veteran has experienced trauma in a different way and each dog will learn to read, to sense, to interpret the trouble signals in their person—whether they are flashbacks, panic attacks, exaggerated startle responses, anger, anxiety, depression, nightmares. There are so many variables.

In my case, for example, I had a real fear of being alone. When you're deployed with a military unit in a combat zone you are never, ever alone. When I first got home and my wife would leave the house, I'd call her two or three times in the first ten minutes after her departure. With Ronnie I am never alone and she and I can read each other instantly. Just as I know when she's uncomfortable, so she senses when things veer "off" for me. She'll come and put her head on my lap. Or if it's at night, she'll hop up on the bed. Sometimes it gets a little crowded up there, since we're trying to accommodate my wife, me, two cats, and Ronnie. But she's responding to a need she feels in me, so we honor that.

There is a lot of research now on how and why some dogs can respond to, even anticipate moments of, human crisis. I don't know if Ronnie can smell stress. I do know that since we are together every hour of every day, we have become a single working unit.

It's odd because we didn't immediately bond. It took about six months for us to really connect. She gravitated initially to my wife and, as we were thinking about it later, we decided this might have had something to do with her female trainers. Apart from her inmate handler, her weekend puppy raisers were female, her advanced trainer, Erin, was female, and Ronnie was accustomed to responding to a female voice. These dogs are unbelievably obedient; she was beautifully trained to do her tasks. She has that whole range of skills: retrieving dropped objects, opening doors, putting out lights. But the emotional bond with her took some time to form.

Of course trauma alert dogs are taught to observe boundaries—to protect a certain kind of space around their person. She doesn't care for people getting in her space because she doesn't like me to feel crowded. So I think there's a certain distance you have to respect, then slowly subtract, as you bond with a trauma alert dog.

I ask Kevin if he has seen any examples of Ronnie's effectiveness in the field while working with veterans and their families.

Absolutely. When I was working primarily in the suicide prevention program, Ronnie accompanied me on interventions and she was often the one who made the crucial difference. I can remember vividly two instances when veterans with weapons were holed up, refusing any treatment. Ronnie went in with me. Her physical presence is calming; she is a source of conversation about something other than the immediate crisis. When she gets a person talking, some of the fear or anger just evaporates. When I asked one veteran, after a long conversation, if he was willing to seek some treatment now, he said, "I will, if Ronnie can come with me."

And in a less dramatic but still important way, she demonstrates everywhere she goes the value an assistance dog can provide for people in all walks of life struggling with a wide range of disabilities. I travel with Ronnie all over the state and beyond and I get questions all the time about the availability of dogs from NEADS. The costs are, of course, a consideration. For civilians, clients are asked to raise $9,500 toward the total expense of their $20,000 dog. But NEADS provides a dog to a qualified veteran free of charge. And that's a large financial

burden for nonprofits like NEADS to handle, especially as the demand requires that they expand these programs. The VA currently reimburses veterans for all the medical expenses associated with their dogs. They don't cover grooming or boarding or food, but they do pay veterinarian expenses. But I'm hoping the day is nearing when the VA will provide the money necessary to raise and train these amazing dogs for any veteran whose life will be changed by an assistance dog.

As we prepare to leave, I ask Kevin what gives him the most pleasure while sharing a life with Ronnie. He thinks for a moment.

I love to watch Ronnie swim. She's amazing in the water. She'll jump off a high embankment or off the side of a boat, range far out beyond any stick I've thrown, and swim as if no boundaries exist. That's her element and it's great to see her so relaxed and free. She's picky; she doesn't like little muddy farm ponds but rather the big stretches of deep water like Lake Sunapee or Lake Champlain.

We were camping in Vermont this past week, and at first Ronnie just looked at me, bewildered, as if to say: "What do I need to do now? What do you need me to do?" I looked at her, patted her on the head, and said, "You just need to be a dog." For a while, since she's used to working all day, every day, she seemed a little lost. But once in the water she's anything but lost. She's home.

It still surprises me to realize that in the thirteen months that I've had her, I've never been without her. She's been a huge part of my healing and recovery and she allows me to help in the healing transitions of other vets. She's come on every work trip, every road trip, every vacation, every medical appointment, every MRI. As long as she can see me, she's happy. And I guess you could say the same for me.

He looks down reflectively at Ronnie, as if turning this idea over in his mind.

Absolutely.

Heather Dawson: Weekend Puppy Raiser

While arranging a meeting with Heather Dawson, whose wonderful website, Tales of a Carnivorous Convict: Life as a Prison Puppy, explores her experiences while socializing three NEADS service dogs, I am startled to hear her say, "Well, I think I can make that time, but I'll have to wait and see when my mom can drive me." This articulate, seasoned puppy trainer and socializer is not yet sixteen. And when she arrives at my house with her newest dog, Kelly, a beautiful Golden Retriever who is in training with Heather in order to shed some shyness, I can see more evidence of maturity beyond her years. Tall, slim, self-possessed, Heather moves with the grace of a dancer and talks to her dog in training in a quiet but clear way. She is completely at home with dogs. Kelly sits obediently at Heather's feet as we talk about the process of being a weekend puppy raiser.

I first became a serious dog lover when I lived in Washington State; our neighbors owned a few dogs and I really bonded with one of their Golden Retrievers. It was from that experience that I learned how much I like training dogs. In 2005 my family moved from Washington to Massachusetts, and I had to leave behind the dog I loved. It was then that I started looking into raising an assistance dog puppy. I found NEADS through a website listing volunteering opportunities, then went to an orientation that drew eleven other people. At the orientation we learned about NEADS' training philosophy, all the rules to follow in structuring a puppy's life, and before we went home we got to work with some of the puppies who were in the nursery. I was definitely interested.

As a weekend raiser we are required to take the puppy out at least three weekends of each month. If you have the commitment, this really presents little problem. Since the puppy is a service dog in training, he or she wears a vest that allows admission almost everywhere. I would often give a store owner a preview that I'd be bringing in a puppy in training, just to avoid any snags, but most were very understanding.

The puppy needs to go everywhere, so that he or she learns how to be comfortable in all sorts of situations. Puppy raisers are required to fill out a weekly online report and NEADS makes suggestions emphasizing the types of places puppies should visit: restaurants, grocery stores, museums, malls, hospitals, train stations, busy streets, pet stores.

I also work on introducing the puppy to all kinds of people so that the puppy associates good things with men and women and children of all sizes and appearances. Even though a puppy raiser's primary responsibility is to socialize the puppy, we also have to teach the dog good manners and practicing basic obedience. Of course the puppies learn their basic commands from the inmate trainers, but a puppy raiser needs to practice these commands while the puppy is in public.

I've been lucky to overlap twice with Jake at Hampshire County House of Correction as we worked with the dogs Ellie and Ronnie. Although I've never met Jake face-to-face, I sense that our training methods are quite similar. Ellie and Ronnie were surprisingly similar in their temperaments. They were both low-key dogs, not as treat-oriented as many Labs I've encountered, and both were bred by Guiding Eyes for the Blind. Ellie was not quite as upbeat in personality and so I used extra positive feedback to keep her motivated and cheerful. Ellie always responded well to praise; she always needed reassurance that she was doing the right thing. But she could be excitable when meeting other dogs, so when I cued her to "Say hello," I toned down my energy, talking to her in a calm voice to lower her excitement. Ellie was matched with a boy who needed help in social situations; I'm sure she'll widen and brighten his contacts with others. And Ronnie made a wonderful match with a returning combat veteran, Kevin Lambert.

Dogs are able to sense your emotions really well. I try to keep that in mind as I train my dogs and socialize them. If you don't surprise them or confuse or hurt them, then their capacities for sensing the mood and emotions of their human partner, one of their greatest gifts, will flower.

Jake Liptak, Prison PUP Program

It's a windy, unusually cold October day and maple leaves swirl in the driveway as we make our way up the hill to the Hampshire County House of Correction. Although the facility is small, a county-run correctional institution, it has participated for seven years in the NEADS Prison PUP Program. Jake Liptak, the inmate handler we're coming to see, has trained three NEADS puppies, two of whom, Ellie and Ronnie, Heather Dawson trained and socialized on weekends. Talking with Jake affords that rare opportunity to learn how puppy training is conducted behind bars and also connects the dots from inmate trainer to weekend puppy raiser to final advanced training and the "match."

After passing through security we meet Jake in a large room filled with rows of chairs, the visitors' room, we're told. Jake, a soft-spoken young man, comes in to greet us with Zack, the most recent black Lab puppy he is working with as a back-up handler. Zack is only twelve weeks old and it's easy to see Jake's patience as he puts the rambunctious puppy through a sit-stay and then gives him permission to greet us. Jake hands me a picture book of photos that Heather has taken of Ellie and Ronnie and begins by talking about a happy memory: a visit from Kevin Lambert and Ronnie.

The day Kevin came to visit was really special for me. Kevin came to thank me for my efforts in training Ronnie and he allowed me to see how well they had bonded, how devoted she is to him. Ronnie started out with a couple of other inmate trainers—before she ended up with me. At first that made her cautious, and I thought she might be confused by all the different trainers and the little changes in each person's style of training. But I think she was just waiting to get it figured out that I was her person now. And when the bond clicked, she was very responsive to learning her commands and her tasks.

Sometimes, you know, guys in here spend a year with a dog and while they hear that the dog has been placed, they don't really have many details. So seeing the client and the dog personally means a great deal. I loved to see the way Ronnie acts around Kevin: she's very obedient, but she's also playful; Kevin even showed me how she will bring his cane to him sometimes and then look up for the smile that follows.

Once Jake gets Zack busy with a chew toy, I ask if he'll describe how an inmate is chosen for this program and how the training unfolds.

If you indicate an interest in this program and you meet the right criteria, the administrator does an evaluation to see if you'd be a good candidate. You have to have the right amount of patience, the commitment, and the right amount of time left here in the facility to complete the job. (They don't like to switch trainers mid-stream, though sometimes that happens.)

Each dog is assigned a trainer and a back-up trainer. Initially I was a back-up trainer, observing the voice commands and hand signals the trainer was using—or maybe it's more accurate to say learning the words and gestures *not* to use. You have to be absolutely consistent in order to avoid confusing the dog. As a back-up you also have some

responsibilities for the dog's care, bathroom breaks, walks, crating at night, feeding. The dogs are crated each night. Here we have four-man rooms with bunk beds on either end and the dog crates in the middle. The puppies are really very good at night. They have their person right with them, other dogs around, and they like their crates—so the nights go pretty smoothly.

Gradually I shifted to becoming a trainer. And Monday through Friday trainers have the puppies 24/7, working on simple commands first, then more complicated commands. The first things you work on are "sit," "down," "shake," and you work with having them maintain eye contact by moving a treat from side to side, hand to hand. As things progress, I'll tackle a task like turning a light switch on and off. I teach the command "touch" first, by having the dog learn to touch my hand with his nose and a treat will follow. Then I'll hold a light fixture in my hand and the dog will learn "nudge," gradually teaching the dog to turn on and off the light switch. As the puppy grows we place the light fixture on a wall, moving it further and further up the wall, so that the puppy has to stretch to reach it. Sometimes we'll put a pen cap sticking out of the switch, so that the puppy has some success hitting the mark. Once the puppy can hit the mark reliably we have the basis for one very important task learned. When you think about it, that's a relatively difficult task to learn: the puppy is standing on her/his hind legs, front paws up against the wall, stretching to hit the switch with his or her nose. It takes lots of repetition and patience. Dogs can also learn to "hit the mark" to open handicapped-accessible doors. And we use the command "tug" to teach a dog to open a door (to which a rope has been attached) and hold it open while a wheelchair or walker goes through.

The "fetch" command is an important one for the dogs to learn reliably. They begin by learning to pick up a light-weight plastic dumbbell, and gradually refine it so that they can pick up more difficult things to handle: keys, a dropped phone, a dropped cane. I've even heard of dogs who can pick up dropped coins. Of course there's always lots of practice on getting a dog to hold a "stay" in any situation, and to climb under a table or chair and remain quiet, almost "invisible."

On weekends, at least three times a month, often all four weekends, the puppy raisers come to take the puppies out into a wider world. I've been lucky to work with Heather Dawson, a young woman who really puts the time and commitment into her dogs. Heather takes her dogs everywhere with her: Ellie even got to New York City! And I could always tell that the dog was a little sharper, a little more attentive, when she got back from a weekend with Heather.

A trainer from NEADS comes for several hours every week to check on our progress. We gather as a group with our dogs and as the trainer works with each team we all listen to benefit from the advice. If there's a problem with a command, or the dog is acting out in any way, or the dog is getting distracted, the NEADS trainer can suggest another approach that almost always works. We have, for example, a big yellow Lab named Romeo who is about to be transferred to another institution

for a few more weeks of training, since he's easily distracted. Romeo has too much to offer to throw in the towel. But even though he responds very well to commands, he'll break eye contact if a tiny bug flies by. He's a big, muscular dog—one who would be a good balance dog, or one who can tug the door open and then hold it open indefinitely. He's too valuable to give up on. So he'll just have to be in school a little longer. Not all dogs can work at exactly the same pace.

I like doing this work, even when it can be a little frustrating, largely because of the prison security that's required. When you have a little puppy who needs to go outside immediately, it's hard to wait until all the doors are properly unlocked. But that just goes with the territory. I appreciate the opportunity to do something that will make such a difference to a disabled person, and, on balance, that's all the motivation I need.

Probably the toughest thing is letting the dog go after being with him or her for a year, day in and day out. For example [Jake looks around the huge visitors' room and nods], one of my jobs is to clean and buff this floor. For a year or more, every time I'd do the floor Ronnie would sit quietly in the corner, watching me work. For weeks after Ronnie was gone when I'd work on the floor I'd automatically glance over in the corner.

But I have happy memories too. You see how all these chairs are lined up and if you look through those lined-up legs you'll see they form a tunnel? Ronnie spotted this tunnel possibility in the placement of the chairs and regardless of whether they were in a line or in a circle, she could run like the wind through the tunnel they created. Had she not become Kevin's best friend, she'd have been in the winner's circle in agility.

Chapter Eight

The Gifts of Being an "Outsider"

Deb Baker and Rusty

Deb Baker and her hearing dog Rusty, a sweet-faced Sheltie/Beagle mix, are something of a legend at L.L. Bean, the famous outdoor clothing and equipment store in Freeport, Maine. Deb works in the Hunting and Fishing department of the giant store and Rusty has his own "work station," directly behind her register. He sits atop an L.L. Bean blanket monogrammed with his name and alerts Deb when someone calls her name or comes up unexpectedly behind her. His major job is to get Deb outside when the fire alarm rings, a task he practices regularly since the store conducts many practice fire alarm drills for the protection of its customers. Not surprisingly, Rusty is a source of keen customer interest; he is alert and appealing, the perfect sidekick for Deb as she greets customers with warmth and courtesy. Small wonder that the line at her register is longer than anyone else's.

We meet Deb and Rusty at their townhouse in Freeport on a crisp September afternoon. Deb ushers us into her dining room; she is animated and energetic, her sentences punctuated with a toss of her long brown hair. Rusty is carrying a baseball cap around, its peak hitting the ground with each step; we'll hear about his baseball fetish later.

Freeport is my home town. And growing up here was pretty normal for me since I grew up in a hearing world. I attended public schools from preschool on. Since I did not lose my hearing until the age of seven, I had the basic building blocks of speech in place, making it easier to talk and to lip-read. I actually thought every child picked up lip-reading while watching *Little House on the Prairie, Wonder Woman,* and *The Six Million Dollar Man.* I picked up this skill before my parents detected something was wrong. My deafness is classified as a "profound hearing loss," which means that sound waves enter my ear canal, go to the brain, but the nervous system that translates the waves into speech is broken. Thus the sound waves remain sound waves as they enter my brain: I hear voices, but cannot distinguish what is being conveyed.

My mother was the first to discover this when I didn't respond to her calling me in for dinner. At first she thought I was being a brat, ignoring her repeated calls. The truth was I no longer could hear her. Of course we went to doctors, but none could discover the cause of my deafness. My condition was deemed "a mystery."

In school I was an easy target for bullies; I was often mocked for "talking funny." Ignoring the bullies was easy enough: whenever I didn't want to listen I simply closed my eyes. But perhaps more troubling was the assumption, seemingly held by most of my teachers, that my deafness made me ineligible for challenging classes. Often I was thrown into the resource room where the work was far too easy for me. I wasn't able to enjoy a full range of normal classes until junior high school and, even then, no interpreters were available until my senior year. I was told I could never learn a language—and I loved languages. I was told I could never lead an independent life or could never work at a high risk job. I was clearly marked as "an outsider." Perhaps it was those very limitations that others were imposing on me that made me bolder, stronger, more determined and intent on pursuing what my real interests were. After high school I packed up my car and drove west alone, cross-country, to take a job at the Grand Canyon and enroll in college, where I mastered several languages. For me, being tagged as an outsider was a real gift; it gave me the incentive to see what I could become. Whenever anybody tells me I can't do something my response is "Really? Let's see about that."

I went to college at Northern Arizona University in Flagstaff. I spent several extra years in college because I wanted to explore many fields of interest that had been denied to me before: geology, art, Japanese, Spanish, Arabic. I found that I could "do languages" after all, since my comprehension came from learning new vocabularies and syntax,

then lip-reading in foreign languages. Of course I'm at a disadvantage conversationally, since I can't hear where the inflections or precise articulations take place in spoken language. But it's fascinating to think and read in another language and that was very satisfying for me.

Theater and history also interested me and I became instantly hooked on British literature: Chaucer, Shakespeare, Milton, Wordsworth, Woolf. My college major combined my love of Shakespeare with my love of theater. Literature that is designed to be presented on stage became my special focus and I loved to explore stage directions and a director's interpretations of the written word. My senior thesis, in fact, presented an alternative interpretation of *Hamlet*, arguing that Hamlet did not finally dissolve into madness, but instead feigned madness, using it as a tactic whereby he could sleuth out his father's murderer. I see the play as a mystery rather than a tragedy. I'm not sure my professor was ever wholly convinced, but I certainly was.

At this point we are interrupted by Rusty, who has raced to the big glass windows, having spotted some squirrels outside. He barks urgently.

"Rusty loves squirrels," Deb explains. "Whether we are hiking in the woods or whether he spots them out the window, they are a major distraction." She pulls him into a sit-stay at her feet.

Sometimes I get a little frustrated at the number of distractions that will set him off: another dog, a kid on a bicycle, my next door neighbor's cat. We've only been together for four months and he's still something of a puppy. And I don't suppose you can expect a dog who is a mix of Beagle and Sheltie to be mute. But I have to pay attention when he signals me. Most of the times when he alerts me he is giving the appropriate signal; he's identifying something he's been trained to bark at. But sometimes it is because he's a social dog who loves people and wants to go out and greet somebody. Mostly I can take it in stride, realizing that this is a learning process. We'll get to be a better and better team as time goes on. We're going to succeed.

After I graduated from college I came back to Freeport and got a job at L.L. Bean. At first I applied for a seasonal job, but later I was asked to

stay year-round. After living alone in my townhouse for half a year, I began to realize how much I needed someone to be my ears and help keep me safe. Several times my neighbors would pound frantically on my door, concerned that my fire alarm had gone off and I didn't seem to notice. Friends regularly reported their disappointment in finding me not at home, when in fact I was upstairs and did not hear them at the door. I knew it was time to regain a full measure of independence and enjoy the freedom of a social life.

Since I had a companion dog, Valleri, in childhood who alerted me to the sounds at home, I realized how even a pet dog could help cue me to the door, my name being called, the fire alarm. Think of the advantages of a specially trained hearing dog. I spent some time looking up assistance dog agencies on the Internet and kept returning to the NEADS website. I was especially drawn to the support system they provide for clients, even after training and graduation are completed. I weighed the benefits of being able to seek help, get answers to questions for the entire lifetime of the match, rather than being handed a dog with a "good luck and happy life" send-off. I put in my application in November, expecting quite a wait, but then things evolved very rapidly. I got Rusty in May and we graduated in June. I think the match was a quick one because Rusty and I suited one another so well.

As I discovered, Rusty had failed at two other adoption attempts. The first family who had picked him up at a shelter had young children who handled him so roughly that the parents returned him to the shelter. The second try was an older couple who simply could not keep up with Rusty's high energy and constant need for exercise.

As it happened, after I started working at L.L. Bean I developed a strong, almost magnetic pull toward the great outdoors. The folks at work would share stories of their weekend adventures and, ever the curious person, I had to check out the hiking and kayaking spots. I hike at Bradbury Mountain in Pownall or in the Camden Hills whenever I have the chance. My favorite spots to kayak are in the Downeast area between Freeport and Harpswell around the islands. From my point of view, I was the perfect person to be matched with Rusty's boundless energy. From Rusty's point of view, well, think of the squirrel opportunities!

In fact, we're about to embark on our first camping venture together. L.L. Bean's personnel have adopted a seventeen-mile stretch of the Appalachian Trail. Every year a number of us go to a pre-arranged campsite where we take our own tents; we have a kitchen tent and all our gear, and over the course of the next three days we enjoy and clean the seventeen-mile stretch of trail that is ours to maintain. I've gone for two years, but this time I'll be taking Rusty with me. Since I have only a one-person tent, I plan to borrow a three-person tent, so that Rusty will be fine and not do any alert barking that isn't necessary. I think we'll pitch the new tent in my parents' back yard and do a trial run before we go.

Deb is wearing a striking necklace, and when Robert asks about it we learn she has a jewelry business, making beautiful beaded necklaces that often take their inspiration from Arizona sunsets and Maine nature preserves. She obligingly brings several

examples of her work to be photographed, adding that she sells her work online and also at times brings her work to fundraisers for Rusty. As Robert snaps some shots, she relates an incident that happened only a few days earlier.

Rusty can be a very serious working dog. Several days ago, while at work, a blood vessel ruptured in my head; my blood pressure and glucose levels plummeted. My co-workers grew alarmed enough to call the paramedics.

Rusty would not leave my side. When they strapped me into a stretcher, he hopped right up on top of me. He was wearing his working vest, of course, and the paramedics were wonderfully supportive, allowing him to ride with me and go right into the ER. The only time he left my side was when my mother had to take him into the hall while I had an MRI. She said he kept sneaking his face around the corner, trying to get a peek at me. Even though I was able to recover reasonably quickly, his presence was a huge help. The ER has always been an unnerving place for me—probably for anybody who cannot

hear. Curtains are suddenly thrown open, people appear unannounced, activity occurs behind you or just out of sight. But with Rusty, I was completely calm. All I have to do is watch his ears. When they twitch or move forward I know somebody is coming, something is about to happen. I'm never taken by surprise.

It may be hard for those in the hearing world to totally grasp the gifts a hearing dog can provide for a deaf person. Rusty is trained to alert me to fire alarms, doorbells or door knocks, the buzzer on the stove, someone calling my name, the alarm clock, the carbon dioxide alarm, a dropped object. Additional sounds that he has learned to alert me to (though he was not specifically trained to identify) include detecting my cell phone vibrator, sensing approaching traffic when I do not, signaling me that others are behind me that I do not see or hear, that neighbors are coming and going, that thunder is approaching. Clearly, Rusty makes life safer for me. But my world is also so much wider, so much richer with Rusty by my side.

He also has a silly side. He loves baseball caps and he carries around one that he stole from a co-worker of mine. Well, recently we were out on a hike and Rusty made a beeline for a particular bush, crawling in under it and digging around furiously. When he emerged, guess what he had in his mouth? A baseball. He insisted we carry it all the way back home. So he's got the cap and the ball. What's next, do you suppose?

Hearing dogs, any kinds of assistance dogs, are not for everybody. I stress to anybody who asks about acquiring one that it takes a real commitment of time, energy, and patience. Typically hearing dogs come from shelters, they are high-energy, and they may have difficult pasts. And as with any dog, you have to be prepared to walk the dog three or four times each and every day: rain, snow, sleet, or hail. (In Maine we get plenty of "weather.") If you're not able or willing to make that commitment, then my recommendation is don't even begin the process.

You know, I think Rusty and I are a good team not simply because his energy and my lifestyle match up well; we also share some parallel past experiences, at least in our early years: abusive behavior, quick judgments from others, an unspoken assumption that we'll never make the grade. We're still working on clear communication skills. But we're on our way to embracing life and all it brings our way. What new sights and sounds do you think Rusty and I will experience when we're on the Appalachian Trail? I can't wait to find out.

Chapter Ten

Balancing and Adjusting

Kristin Hartness Law and Bronson

We're eager to meet Kristin Hartness Law at her office on the NEADS campus, since not only was she one of the first recipients of a walker/balance dog, trained at NEADS in 2001, she is the executive director of Canines for Disabled Kids. CDK is an independently organized and funded program that focuses on placing assistance dogs with children between the ages of six and eighteen to help them gain greater independence as they cope with autism spectrum, Asperger's syndrome, hearing impairments, or other physical disabilities.

Her office, located in a brown ranch-style house in a wooded area close to the NEADS campus, also serves, in some instances, as housing space for children and their parents when they come to train with their new assistance dogs. It's easy to understand why kids would feel comfortable in this setting, with its brick fireplace and walls lined with photos of smiling kids and their dogs, success stories all.

Kristin's service dog, Bronson, is as impressive as Kristin's credentials. Neither Robert nor I have seen a Smooth-coat Collie in the flesh before, and Bronson is every bit as elegant as his breed's representatives in the Westminster Dog Show. He is sable and white, with expressive eyes and a sculpted, muscular build. Kristin explains that one of the reasons this breed is ideal for walker/balance purposes is that they have very little "roll" in their shoulders, the area where the harness is placed. The resulting steadiness provides an undeviating support "platform" that allows the dog and partner to move forward smoothly and with confidence. Kristin settles Bronson at her feet and begins by describing her long connection with the NEADS program.

I had a very early point of contact when this program was in its infancy. The program that was to evolve into NEADS began in 1976, when some students at Holliston Junior College began to test and

work with dogs that could be trained to become the "ears" for the deaf. My father, who learned sign language, was an instructor at that time teaching veterinary technicians who, in turn, were working with these dogs. I was the little kid, running around asking too many questions and distracting the dogs. Although my father took on a different career path later and the program evolved into a much more comprehensive mission, I had a very early introduction to assistance dogs and their potential.

By the age of sixteen I began to experience the symptoms of what would later be diagnosed as MS. And by the year 2000 I was looking to find ways to combat the gradual erosions of my independence. I had a friend who was a puppy raiser for NEADS and she said, "They are developing a new kind of dog at NEADS, a walker/balance dog. I'm not entirely sure if a dog can offer the kind of assistance that will help you, but if I were you I'd look into it."

And so I did—and was accepted as one of the first very small group of folks to work with these special dogs. On April 1, 2001, I received my first dog, Laddie, a tri-colored Smooth-coat Collie, now pushing twelve and at home, fully retired. Of course nobody was certain when I got Laddie how well this partnership might work. I can remember thinking to myself, well, even if Laddie can pick up things I drop or carry things I need to bring with me in his backpack, then that would be very useful. But after I got Laddie I went from falling at least twice a week to falling maybe twice in six months. He restored some crucial independence that I had lost to MS. It will always, of course, take me longer to accomplish some tasks than a nondisabled person, but Laddie reduced my need to depend on family and friends for many of the basics: I could walk with a much greater degree of safety, Laddie could fetch dropped things, he could bark on command for help if I did fall and need assistance getting up, I could travel with him rather than having to ask a friend or family member to accompany me everywhere. I'm sure you've heard this before from other NEADS clients: being dependent on others for some basic necessities of life robs you of self-esteem. It can be emotionally crippling. With Laddie I have the luxury of relating to my family and friends as family and friends, not caregivers. Laddie was a superb working partner and I started to tell everybody about this huge benefit I had received. I was asked to do some public speaking for NEADS, then later hired to do the public tours of the NEADS facility.

The Canines for Disabled Kids, an offshoot of NEADS but an independent entity in its own right, began in 1998; very few assistance dog programs were offering dogs for children under the age of twelve. CDK saw the need and worked to fill it. When CDK was looking for a new executive director, Sheila O'Brien, then CEO of NEADS, came to me saying she'd like to recommend me for the position, if I was amenable. I was delighted with this new opportunity and have served as director for the last eight years. The programs work closely together, except that the focus at CDK is on kids. We provide scholarships for dogs trained at NEADS to children with a wide range of physical disabilities. We also work very hard at public education, making schools and communities more welcoming to children with assistance dogs.

We want to make the sight of a child and service dog as commonplace as wearing glasses. Nobody questions you if you walk into a school or a restaurant or a mall wearing glasses. Nobody asks you to take the glasses off. Well, our goal is to have service dogs as easily accepted as a pair of glasses, a normal, commonplace piece of assistance that everybody recognizes and accepts.

Like NEADS, we are a nonprofit organization relying on donations and fundraisers. Since we do lots of work in the schools we get wide support from school children who organize penny collections or have baked goods sales and donate the proceeds to us. Some of that money is used for education and some we put toward scholarships to help families pay for their dogs. I travel a great deal in my work (and yes, Bronson flies with me, lying at my feet). I got back a few days ago from a trip to Texas, speaking to a large conference of veterinarians, and soon I'll be flying to Los Angeles to speak in a number of schools. Getting out the word, nationally and internationally, is a vital part of my job.

Since Kristin is the first person we've encountered who has had the experience of retiring one service dog and acquiring a second, I ask her if she'll describe that process.

Not everyone can retire their first assistance dog and keep it in their own home. Their disability may not permit them to care for an aging dog in addition to keeping a second working dog. And although NEADS recommends keeping a retired dog whenever possible, sometimes that just won't work.

I was lucky in that Bronson and Laddie got along very well. Both had been trained in the same program, so they understood the same commands and they had been taught to accept other dogs in their space. We did take the time to introduce them, to allow them to adjust to one another's presence, and to ensure that they were respectful of one another.

At first Bronson deferred to the older dog, Laddie. But in a very

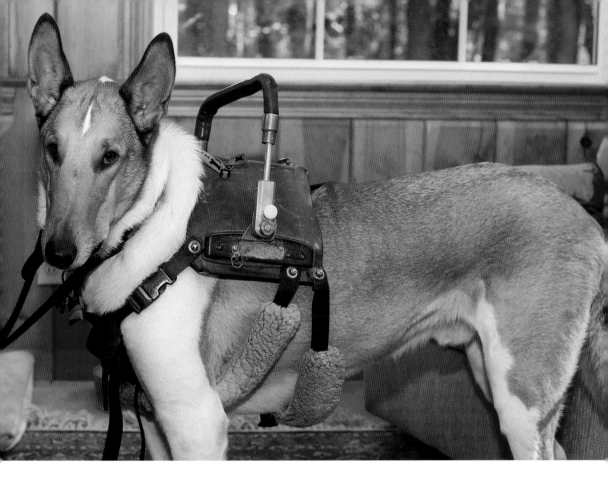

natural way, over time, they made those "pack adjustments" that dogs make when living together. I'm in the number 1 slot, Bronson is 2, and Laddie is 3.

I think Laddie was really ready to allow Bronson to do the work, so there wasn't conflict or jealousy there. What did happen, initially, was that when Bronson and I would prepare to leave for the day, Laddie wanted to come too. At that time, I luckily had enough flexibility in my schedule to accommodate him. When Laddie walked us expectantly to the door, what I chose to do was to take both dogs on a brief errand, like a visit to my mother's house around the corner, or I would take both dogs into the bank to make a deposit. The bank teller there adores Laddie and he'd get a treat just like Bronson. Then I'd circle back home, drop Laddie at the house, and he'd be fine for the rest of the day. After a few months Laddie just accepted that he wouldn't be going along each time we left for work, and he adjusted his routine accordingly.

I probably should add that I own four dogs: the two Collies, a Fabulous Flunkout, a Sheltie who developed eye problems very early in the training process and is now almost blind, and Emmit, another woman's retired service dog. (She passed away.) So there's plenty of company at home and they all get along well. I've heard it's common for a retired service dog to retain one or two tasks that they love to do. Emmit loves to fetch. So that's his special task at home—and it gives Bronson some relief. Laddie likes to take off my socks. So he'll take off one sock and Bronson, the other. It's quite the integrated home team.

There is very little difference between Laddie and Bronson in their skill levels. Because they trained in the same program and are the same breed, they are very consistent in the way they perform. So I faced very few adjustments on that front. They do differ in their personalities. When Laddie would meet the world as a working dog, he'd essentially say, "Hey, it's the world. Do I care? Nope." Bronson meets the world saying, "Hey, world, I am here. I *am* the world." I'm lucky, since my MS has progressed, to be able to stay with my service dogs. Both have been trained to adjust with me, to assist me as my needs change. While they differ in temperaments and, now, in physical strength, I am so grateful that they can continue to accompany me on my life's journey.

As we prepare to leave I ask Kristin if she sees particular challenges as NEADS and CDK look to the future.

Well, I think it's important for people to understand why CDK exists as an independent organization, not as a mouthpiece for NEADS or any other training organization. Although our programs are closely related, we maintain our own budget, raise our own money, and offer free educational programs in schools to help familiarize students who may not yet have had much exposure to assistance dogs. I see CDK functioning in the role of guidance counselor rather than recruiter, a role that helps sort out options for a family who is making a crucial decision. We try to help a family determine if an assistance dog is right for their child: At what age is it best to apply for a dog? How will a dog help with the specific needs of that child? How will this new "tool" fit into the larger family unit? As we expand our program and enlarge our educational efforts, we want to retain our independence, which after all is one measure of our credibility.

But expansion in this tough economy affects both CDK and NEADS; I suppose it's fair to surmise that it affects all nonprofits. And I think each of our programs, in trying to address the needs of the future, has to keep in mind the big picture. Some programs that train assistance dogs for kids focus on one specialty—seizure dogs, or dogs for kids with autism. And that's fine as long as they are transparent about their mission. But NEADS and CDK have always been broader in their reach. Those of us who have been associated with these programs for some time feel keenly the demands of that balancing act. For example, it may be true that the need for service dogs for returning combat vets has increased dramatically over the past seven or eight years. While we want to pay attention to that, we have to be mindful that the need for service dogs for civilians with other disabilities has not decreased. Or, more specifically in my field, while it's important to recognize that the demand for dogs to assist children with autism has increased dramatically, the need for dogs to help children with other disabilities has not decreased. We want to help as many people as we can, but we also want to be mindful of our original mission. And sometimes that requires lots of weighing and balancing.

She looks over and smiles at Bronson.

Balancing and adjusting: that's my life story.

Chapter Eleven

100 Percent Special

Jake Greendale and Basket

Robert and I wind around the wooded outskirts of Holliston, Massachusetts, en route to talk with the Greendale family and meet Jake Greendale and his service dog, Basket. Jake's mother, Liz, has told me to watch for a horse farm, an across-the-street marker for their driveway. But horses seem common in this neighborhood of large lots, multiple outbuildings, and big, comfortable clapboard houses. When we pull into the yard we're greeted not only by Jake and Basket, but by Liz and her husband, Alan, Jake's older brother, Alan Jr., eleven, and younger sister, Riley, four. Clearly, Basket doesn't lack for playmates or stimulation. Liz confides, "Basket is supposed to be Jake's dog—and respond in a primary way to him. She does, of course, but when you have other young children who also love to run and play with the dog, it's only natural . . . " (and she raises her hands in a gesture of the inevitable).

Jake, an animated boy of ten with a thick mop of chestnut hair, introduces Basket by demonstrating some of the commands and tricks Basket can perform. The responsive black Lab executes a "sit-stay" on either side of Jake, a roll-over, and an "under" command (making herself quite inconspicuous under a wooden love seat) as Liz begins to tell the story of acquiring the dog.

I heard of NEADS through a friend who also has a son with autism. We were looking for help with one particular behavior Jake exhibited that made me feel insecure in taking him along with me to malls and crowded public places. Jake had the tendency, without provocation, to run off. I'd look up from tending to Riley, for example, and suddenly Jake would be nowhere in sight—a panic-inducing situation for any parent, further complicated by the fact that although Jake knew his name, sometimes he would neither give it nor respond to it. I thought

if acquiring a dog could help with that behavior, that alone would be worth the time and trouble and training. That alone would offer Jake greater safety and me greater freedom and peace of mind. But as it turned out, Basket could do much more for Jake.

So I contacted NEADS and went for an interview with Kathy Foreman. She was both very gentle and very searching in her questions, taking the time to learn about our specific needs, what kind of a temperament a dog would need to have to fit into our family structure, and our commitment to the long term care of the dog. We were approved in July and I was told that it might be a year before a match could be made. But in four months NEADS called, telling us about Basket, and inviting us to the two-week training session. Basket came home with us in November, right before Thanksgiving. We've had her more than a year now.

Brian Jennings and Dan Ouellette were our trainers. I believe Basket was in the Prison PUP Program at the Gardner facility and originally came from Guiding Eyes for the Blind, where she had been trained as a service dog. So she had the full repertoire of commands. In some ways that enhanced the fit for Jake. He is very sensitive to loud noises and Basket never barks except on command. Even Basket's "failings"—that she was a little too friendly, a little too gregarious to be a seeing-eye dog—worked to Jake's advantage, since he could use Basket as an ice-breaker to enter conversations or social situations more easily. And Basket warmed to all the kids in our family, rather than forming an exclusive bond with Jake.

Two other young boys with autism trained with us and it was interesting to watch Dan's effectiveness with children who exhibited various strengths and needs. It's a hard two weeks, because you have to absorb so much in such a short period of time. But Dan had a way of impressing on each boy what was of utmost importance to him. With Jake he emphasized the importance of always holding Basket's leash—never letting it go. And that became not only a physical anchor for Jake, but in some ways an emotional anchor as well. Jake could enter crowds firmly tethered to Basket. If he had the responsibility for his dog, he could not suddenly disappear.

Dan also impressed on Jake the importance of caring for Basket—feeding her and cleaning up after her. And Jake has accepted that responsibility, carrying it out faithfully. He doesn't always like the way it smells, so he pulls his shirt over his nose, but day in and day out, he does it. And that care, of course, reinforces the bond with the dog.

Jake is verbal and high functioning as you can see, but during the trainings I could observe some of the other tasks that could be used to help more severely challenged children. I think it's fair to say that for most children with autism the world is too loud. Rather than being able to choose those sights and sounds and stimuli layered into everyday experiences like going to the supermarket, or to a mall, or even to a school playground, an autistic child experiences a barrage of noises that hit with equal force. This can create confusion, disorientation, and sometimes fear. The parent or friend accompanying the child faces a daunting set of challenges, for in the blink of an eye the child can dart away.

Service dogs can be of enormous value, calming a child in a moment of sensory overload, locating a child who has managed to dart away,

anchoring a child who is instructed to "hold on to that leash" at all costs.

Of course autism's symptoms can vary widely (which is why children are said to be on the "autism spectrum"). But there are some hallmark behaviors, many of which a service dog can help relieve. A service dog can help interrupt repetitive behavior, soothe nightmares, provide a comforting touch throughout the night, and, perhaps most importantly, prove to be a faithful, loving companion in a world that can seem a lonely and sometimes downright hostile place.

When we were in training with Basket, Jake learned that he must make eye contact and speak clearly in order to communicate with his dog. Not coincidentally, those are social skills he needs to practice daily. And caring for the dog teaches patience and responsibility, just as romping with Basket in the yard or splashing around in the pool helps with coordination. Dogs thrive on routines, as do many children with autism. Creating patterns in daily life benefits Basket and benefits Jake.

In fact, after Basket brought greater attention and greater safety to our world we were able to enjoy a trip to Disney World, enjoying with Basket almost all of the various parks. Basket could ride many of the rides with us and the only park that bothered her was Animal Kingdom. I think there were way too many smells for her to get comfortable and she barked and barked. Basket is a good-looking dog and many kids at Disney World would come over to Jake in order to see her. Talking about the dog created the kind of social bridge that often had been missing before. On balance, we had a fine time and this would not have been a trip we could have imagined before Basket was in our lives.

As Liz has been talking Jake has brought from his room a number of small airplanes for Robert to inspect. Evidently, he has a large collection of models of various military fighter planes and his father tells us, in a quiet aside, "Jake has a special interest in planes: he's studied them and knows quite a lot about them." Alan was an officer in the National Guard, Corps of Engineers, and is also a student of military history. Jake has picked up his interest in planes and tanks from his dad and also from watching programs on the Military History Channel. As luck would have it, Robert studied engineering in college and did design work on some of the planes Jake is describing. He puts down his camera, and briefly, they form a small mutual admiration society.

Mary Greendale, Jake's grandmother, drops by for a visit during our conversation. Basket greets her by rolling over as a cue for a belly rub. Clearly, Mary is a star not only with the kids but with the dog in the family. She's something of a star for me as well, since I've recently read her moving description of Jake and Basket in Bay State Parent *magazine, written in honor of Autism Awareness Month.*

"Jake understands some of his limitations as a highly-functioning autistic," she observes. "He says, 'I am 10 percent intelligent in friendship,' yet he knows too that he is very intelligent about nature, very creative, and 100 percent special. Our family knew how desperately Jake wanted friends, how much he wants to be a good friend, but children with autism often struggle with the nuances of building relationships. In Basket, Jake has a best friend. And our family will be forever grateful."

As we turn to leave Robert calls out to Jake, "Hey Jake, what's the best thing about Basket?"

The reply is swift: "Everything. She's the perfect puppy."

Chapter Twelve

Life Does Triumph

Cynthia Crosson and Dandi

The First Congregational Church, UCC, established in 1771, with its soaring white steeple and beautifully carved pews, seems the picture-postcard image of a New England church, nestled in the sugar maple–lined streets of the quintessential New England village of Whately, Massachusetts. We have come to interview Cynthia Crosson, who became minister of this church three years ago, fulfilling an aspiration to enter the ministry that dates from her college years. The arc of her professional and personal experience threads through years as a clinical social worker, a college professor, a wife and mother, an author of eight highly respected books in the field of child abuse and child welfare, and most recently the co-founder of the TAD (Trauma Alert Dog) program at NEADS and psychiatric consultant to the program.

Some people have the gift of inspiring trust, and with her steady gaze and encouraging smile, Cynthia Crosson is one. She seems equally at home in the busy corridors of NEADS or in the vaulted sanctuary of the Whately church, always accompanied by her service dog for ministry, Dandi, a dark-haired Shih Tzu, whose diminutive crimson NEADS vest accentuates his distinctive trot. While Dandi has been known to have a few mischievous moments—as when he partook of his "first communion" by snatching up a piece of blessed bread Cynthia accidentally dropped during a communion service—he is another example of the beautifully trained, responsive helpmate dog that is the NEADS trademark.

I ask Cynthia if she'll describe her path to the ministry and also those life forces that led her to establish the TAD program.

I grew up on the West Coast, the only child of an Episcopal minister. My father had a large church in California and I spent my early years there, probably more immersed in church activities than many

youngsters who had brothers and sisters to play with might. My father had always wanted to be a writer, however, and when I was twelve my dad "retired" to write. Homesick for the East Coast, my family moved to Massachusetts. I went to college with the intention of becoming a minister, taking a double major in religion and drama. But that was the mid-'60s: the Episcopal Church had only recently begun to ordain women and, if a woman priest was married, all the logistics of having a husband and potentially a family were in the process of being figured out. I discovered I'd need to be a trailblazer, and that really didn't suit my temperament, at least at that time.

I took a look at several other career options and decided to settle on social work. After some years as a social worker with families and children, I completed a master's in social work at the University of Connecticut. I joined the faculty of Fitchburg State College, where I taught for twenty-four years. During these years I finished my doctorate at the University of Massachusetts and also wrote a number of books

on child welfare, specializing in child abuse, its signs and signals, how to detect it, and what measures one can take to prevent against it. Do you know the poem by Robert Frost, "The Road Not Taken"? I've often thought of my career choices as limned by that poem—since I chose the road to social work, which served me well, but inexorably came to the other path, the ministry, much later in life.

During these years I had married and we had three sons: Chay, James (known as Jamie), and Andrew. By the time Jamie was in high school I knew the marriage was, as they say, irretrievably broken, and we divorced during Jamie's senior year. That was a turbulent time for all of us, but it appeared to exact a particular toll on Jamie. He seemed to be unable to decide whether or not he wanted to go to college and, if so, where and what course of study to pursue. So when he came to me one evening to announce that he wanted to go into the service, the Army Rangers Airborne, I was perplexed. While both of my other two sons are perfectly wonderful, Jamie and I had been especially close, perhaps because we both valued the spiritual dimensions in life. Traditional religious expression interested Jamie less than the ancient forms of worship, those embedded in nature, and he was also drawn to Native American history and spiritual practice. In my mind I couldn't quite balance the military with this highly spiritual young man, but he seemed so enthusiastic about joining that I endorsed his plan. He signed up for eight years and, after the requisite training, was sent to Bosnia on a "peacekeeping mission."

He wrote deeply moving letters describing some of his experiences in Bosnia and I could see that he was grappling with some of the deeper moral and ethical issues that war raises.

In one letter I remember vividly he wrote: "None of it makes sense. There are no good guys and no bad guys. The newspapers make such a big deal about the Serbs killing the Muslims, but neglect to say that the Muslims have no qualms about killing the Serbs either. Is it really worth killing someone simply because they are of a different religion or have different values? How could anyone look into the innocent eyes of Bosnian children and see anything but the reflection of how wrong this fighting is? It would be enough to lose hope unless you bear witness to the fact that, regardless of the sometimes heinous and destructive nature of man, life does triumph." He met many of the victims of ethnic cleansing and wrote poignantly of a young woman who had been raped, had borne the child who was the consequence of that violent act, and yet had made the conscious decision to love and nurture the child as "a gift of joy."

I think he also saw some unspeakable things. He was required to dig up mass graves and rebury the bodies, or to recover body parts of victims literally blown apart by bombs. When he came home on leave he was different: he was depressed, he had trouble sleeping, he had sudden anger—all of the symptoms that I, as a longtime therapist, should have recognized as the classic symptoms of Post Traumatic Stress Disorder. But I didn't.

Jamie was disturbed enough by what he had seen that he decided to serve his last four years in the Reserves. He was stationed for a time in Kansas, where he met a young woman with whom he began what would become a tortured and destructive relationship. Soon he got a call from the military saying he was on standby for deployment to Iraq. When they call you for a deployment in Iraq you have to appreciate that they say, "Draw up a will: you're going to Iraq." He drew up his will, and he also looked for work while he endured three postponements of his orders. No employer would take a chance on somebody who could be called up at any time, so he was, essentially, in limbo. Finally, he got word that he would not be needed in Iraq. One morning shortly thereafter, he and I had a long talk, one where he said to me pointedly, "You are my lifeline." He talked about returning to college and he seemed less precarious than he had in a long time. The next morning, he had left the house, and the following morning the police knocked on my door to say, "Your son is dead."

The circumstances are tangled, but evidently the young woman with whom he had been involved called him. She had taken up with another man and was, we think, asking for Jamie's protection. He went to her, scuffled with the man, the gun went off—slightly injuring the man. And according to police reports Jamie turned the gun on himself.

I've come to understand that I'll never know the true facts of that night. But for the longest time what was even more difficult to tolerate was that I didn't recognize the symptoms of PTSD, nor could I forget the sentence, "You are my lifeline."

Whether he killed himself or whether he willingly went into a situation he knew was volatile really adds up to the same thing. I came to understand his death as a suicide.

Since I had grown up with dogs and knew them to be special agents of healing, and since I was in seminary at the time, I applied to NEADS for a ministry dog. Dandi had originally been in training as a service dog, but he was frightened of loud noises, most particularly the sudden loud clanging when the prison doors slam shut at night. So although he could not be used as a service dog, he could be placed as a ministry dog. He has found his calling and been incredibly healing to me, to my NEADS clients, and to many of my parishioners.

In 2007 Sheila O'Brien, who knew of my experience in treating people with PTSD, asked if I could work to help develop a program at NEADS that would address the growing number of returning veterans who, in addition to physical disabilities, suffered from PTSD. And so I began my reading and research, shifting my thinking about PTSD from abused children and their abusers to soldiers in constant danger, night and day, for months and months at a time.

I began to work with Kathy Foreman, the wonderful client coordinator at NEADS, and Brian Jennings, the equally wonderful senior trainer at NEADS. I revised the NEADS application form to reflect more of the psychology of the applicant and shifted the medical history so that it included a psychiatric history as well. I listed the symptoms of PTSD and put them on a chart. And then we brainstormed about what kind of dog might be needed, and what kinds of services a dog could provide to help alleviate these symptoms. Erin Wylie, another talented trainer, joined us, and together the four of us created a series of tools that could assist returning soldiers as they coped with the symptoms of PTSD through the use of service dogs.

The veterans in the TAD program follow essentially the same procedures as any NEADS applicant, with some variations: they apply, they are interviewed (but by all of us), they are observed with some dogs, we look at their support system at home and their level of commitment to a dog. Since they will be meeting as a group periodically, we also look at their capacities to mesh as a group. The trainers find the right dogs for them and they come for their two-week in-house training period.

As an agency, we pride ourselves on our ability to match a dog to a specific person. For the TAD program this becomes especially important. For example, one fellow who plans to pursue a career that will keep him outdoors much of the time needed a big, sturdy, energetic Lab who could handle all kinds of weather conditions. Another veteran, who is struggling with significant physical disabilities, required a stable, quiet dog who can assist him when he falls, do specific tasks, and generally be alert to ensure his well-being. Beyond this careful matching and some additional training to accommodate the specific needs of the

veteran, the dogs do the rest, often intuitively.

The program is still in the exploratory stages as we seek to determine if the placement of dogs for combat-related PTSD will really be beneficial. But we have already come to believe that it is a marvelous way to help our veterans. We have seen, for example, the man who was so dependent on his wife that she was beginning to feel stifled learn to depend on his service dog, so that now he is quite comfortable being alone. We have seen a man who never went out of his house use his dog to aid him in becoming more involved in his religious community and his neighborhood. His young children are thrilled—not only by the presence of a friendly and beautiful dog, but because they now have their father back again. We have seen a veteran gain the strength, through the presence of his dog, to return to a PTSD therapy program that he may have needed, but had not yet had the courage to face.

The veterans call their dogs "my battle buddy," the one who always "has my back." In combat, a "battle buddy" was always with them, then cruelly stripped away when their duty was over. As the dogs supply that vital presence, thoughts of suicide and alcohol abuse diminish. "Who would take care of my dog if I couldn't?," they worry. And since PTSD not only damages the veteran who suffers from it but also those who love and care for that veteran, families rejoice when a real measure of stability and health returns. One of our TAD vets puts it succinctly: "My dog doesn't take away my PTSD. She gives me a better way to cope with it."

Cynthia looks down and smiles at Dandi, who is vigorously preparing his bed for a nap. "As I work with these veterans through TAD, I see Jamie and I am convinced that, had he had a service dog to help with his PTSD, he would still be with us today. He propels me in this work. It is how he and I make sense of his death." She takes a long pause.

I told you earlier that Jamie was fascinated by Indian lore: he had the habit of leaving feathers for me in the most unlikely places—on my desk chair, in a book I was reading. One afternoon, as I was coming out of NEADS, feeling pretty encouraged about how things were coming together in the TAD program, I looked down, just steps from where my car was parked, and, seemingly out of nowhere, there was a bright and beautiful feather.

Epilogue

Pistons

Walking a dog—or to put it more accurately, walking while companioned by a dog—has been a daily ritual for most of my adult years. Since I've lived in northwestern Pennsylvania and western Massachusetts, regions famous for challenging and rapidly changing weather, mine is a routine some might not find very appealing. Yet I know I'd be infinitely poorer without these daily walks.

For one thing, you see, really see, parts of the day many others miss. If, for example, you work a day job, as I did for many years in Pennsylvania—one requiring me to arrive at my office by 8:30 and not leave campus before about 4:30—my dog walks often corresponded with sunrises and sunsets, those ruby and burnt sienna–streaked skies that evolve and devolve so rapidly that one has to be attentive, looking skyward in anticipation, in order not to miss them.

After moving to Massachusetts, I discovered late-afternoon autumn light in New England, with its low angling intensity, can also be spectacular. It casts diagonals across farm fields and barns, splashing the harrows and rough-sawn barn boards with radiance. Such piercing illumination even occasions warnings on the Massachusetts Turnpike—signs announcing to drivers, ALERT: Sun Glare. But for the dog saunterer, it is simply one of nature's more acute ways of seeing.

Dogs experience the natural world through all of their senses, of course, not simply sight, and a walk in the woods can provide a smorgasbord of sensory riches: the musky, earth-rich odor of decomposing leaves, pine needles, and loam, the rhythmic honking of migratory geese as they seek out the river's compass, the taste and texture of dew or hoar frost on the grass. To walk with a dog whose sensory capacities far exceed our own is to sharpen the edges of our own perceptions. Dogs are great noticers and they signal a wealth of concrete information and beauty we'd otherwise miss.

Dogs are who they are, grounded by what they experience, without pretense or guile. They live in the fullness of the present moment, like models of the value of mindfulness. Their capacities for love and trust and joy often surpass our own and while they have spent thousands of years as they have been domesticated watching our behavior, we, too, watch their behavior and are changed by it.

As Robert and I have crisscrossed New England gathering the stories and the images of the remarkable people and equally remarkable dogs who appear in these pages, I've thought about this interactive human-canine bond in a more complexly layered way. If few of the sixty-five million dog owners in the United States would dispute the notion that a dog presence in their lives enhances their emotional and physical well-being, how much deeper is the bond between an assistance dog and his or her human partner?

Acknowledging the depth of this bond, truly "another language," is one of the implicit narratives in this book. It is startling to enter this world and see it in action, even if remaining something of an outsider, at best a witness or scribe. Equally startling is the explosion of interest in the value and potential uses of service dogs; many new cutting-edge training programs are now available or will be in the near future. NEADS has been in the forefront of developing programs that utilize the time and training talents of prison inmates and that place balance and trauma alert dogs with combat vets who have suffered injuries in the line of duty. Other assistance dog training centers across the United States are developing programs that will benefit people who suffer from seizures or very young children with a wide range of physical and/or developmental disorders.

Perhaps, not surprisingly, all of the teams we interviewed and photographed recognize that they are their own best ambassadors. They field questions every time they appear in public or in their workplaces, they actively volunteer in hospitals, rehab facilities, nursing homes, churches, fundraisers, schools, libraries. They add their creative energy and insight to widening the circle of awareness, so that others who might benefit from a service dog see that potential demonstrated in action.

There is an inherent risk when a writer sets out to compose a book titled "Another Language." I'm reminded of the caution Samuel Johnson issued when he said, "If one experiences the unutterable, he'd be well advised not to utter it." The impossibility of finding verbal equivalents for the powerful bonds I was witnessing prompted me to step out of the way, allowing the narrators to speak in their own voices. And I became increasingly grateful for Robert's artistic eye, often capturing feelings that lie beyond language itself.

My father loved to relate the story of Charles Franklin Kettering, the prolific inventor who was instrumental in designing the internal combustion engine, thereby revolutionizing the modern automobile industry. Kettering was, as the story goes, trying to explain the workings of his piston-ignition apparatus to an engineer, a man who also held a prestigious academic chair. When Kettering finished the explanation the professor drew himself up to his full height and said, scoffingly, "That, sir, contradicts all the laws of engineering, and I, sir, am an engineer." To which the Scottish-born Kettering quietly replied, "Aye, but have you ever been a piston?"

The feeling of being a piston, the active agent helping to power the whole engine, is the closest analogy I can find to describe what ignites the bond between service dogs and their human companions, or what fuels the mission of a place like NEADS—where nobody talks about "having a job," but rather about "having a passion."

To touch these stories is to feel their pulse.

Acknowledgments

My primary thanks go to Kathy White, Bob Swain, Beth Lewis, Heidi Martin-Coleman, Sunny Goodwin, Alexis Courneen, Kevin Lambert, Heather Dawson, Jake Liptak, Deb Baker, Cynthia Crosson, Kristin Hartness Law, and Jake Greendale and family. I'm grateful for their willingness to participate in emotionally complex conversations; in telling stories that exemplify the diverse ways an assistance dog can make a pivotal difference in someone's life and life-work, they were honest, articulate, and often very funny. One happy consequence of researching this book was acquiring a very special new group of friends.

I received a great deal of support and practical assistance from various staff members at NEADS. I'd like to thank the former CEO of NEADS, Sheila O'Brien, the current CEO, Gerry DeRoche, COO Candi Hitchcock, trainers Dan Ouellette and Christy Bassett, Communications Director John Moon, who arranged all of my initial contacts with his special brand of energy, and especially Kathy Foreman, the client coordinator, and Cynthia Crosson, the co-founder and psychiatric consultant of the TAD program at NEADS. NEADS is an inspiring place to visit and surely one major reason is the character of the people it employs.

I had extraordinary luck in landing with publisher Sarah Bauhan. She gravitated to these stories and images almost immediately and, together with editor Jane Eklund and art director Henry James, created a perfect home for them. And my abiding thanks to Barry Moser, whose generosity in support of this project is as deep and inventive as his talent.

Pam Peterson, the most imaginative first reader one could ever hope to find, supported the writing of this book in all the ways that matter. Once again, she knows my debt—and I hope the depth of my gratitude. Tim Mullen and Mary Jeanne Mullen, "my kids," buoyed me through some challenging times for our family as this book was composed—and they contributed the money to name a NEADS service dog in my honor, the birthday gift of a lifetime.

Finally, heartfelt thanks to Robert Floyd, my artistic partner in this endeavor. Robert has the rare gift of capturing, in a spontaneous moment, the spirit of a canine-human bond. He does it unobtrusively, without fuss or formal arranging. He is also a true bon vivant, one who views each assignment as a new adventure. We often pulled out of the driveway laughing, and singing a slightly off-key version of "On the Road Again."